Visible Learning: Lesson Planning

In *Visible Learning: Lesson Planning*, John Hattie and Klaus Zierer make it easy to implement the world-famous *Visible Learning*® research into the bedrock of teaching and preparation – lesson planning.

By implementing the *Visible Learning*® data in everyday teaching, this book provides a practical guide to lesson planning that is unique and objective. Important planning steps are explained and described using example lessons in several different subjects. Success criteria are described, and simple strategies to implement, intervene with, and evaluate lessons effectively are provided including, critically, how to switch from surface to deep learning and back again. This book:

- combines the largest body of empirical educational research to date (now informed by more than 2,100 meta-analyses and implementation in thousands of classrooms globally) with the everyday task of lesson planning
- includes empirical research on teaching and learning as well as theoretical studies on lesson planning
- is orientated toward the phases of analysis, planning, implementation, and evaluation of a lesson
- illustrates theoretical principles and empirical research results using a specific lesson
- provides advice for learners, parents, school administrators, and teachers
- offers numerous opportunities for consolidation through in-depth tasks at the levels of surface understanding and deep understanding
- follows evidence-based criteria for the successful professionalization of teachers

This powerful and essential guide, which includes model plans, exercises, and checklists, will show any school how to implement Hattie's research to maximize student success.

John Hattie is Emeritus Laureate Professor at the Graduate School of Education, University of Melbourne, Australia. He is one of the world's best-known and most widely read education experts, and his *Visible Learning* series of books have been translated into 29 different languages and have sold over 2 million copies.

Klaus Zierer is Professor of Education at the University of Augsburg, Germany, and Associate Research Fellow of the ESRC-funded Centre on Skills, Knowledge and Organisational Performance (SKOPE) at the University of Oxford, UK. He has translated *Visible Learning* into German and published several works with John Hattie.

Visible Learning: Lesson Planning

An Evidence-Based Guide for Successful Teaching

John Hattie and Klaus Zierer

LONDON AND NEW YORK

Designed cover image: © Dani Pasteau

First edition published 2025
by Routledge
4 Park Square, Milton Park, Abingdon, Oxon, OX14 4RN

and by Routledge
605 Third Avenue, New York, NY 10158

Routledge is an imprint of the Taylor & Francis Group, an informa business

© 2025 John Hattie and Klaus Zierer

The right of John Hattie and Klaus Zierer to be identified as authors of this work has been asserted in accordance with sections 77 and 78 of the Copyright, Designs and Patents Act 1988.

All rights reserved. No part of this book may be reprinted or reproduced or utilised in any form or by any electronic, mechanical, or other means, now known or hereafter invented, including photocopying and recording, or in any information storage or retrieval system, without permission in writing from the publishers.

Visible Learning® is a trademark of Corwin Press, Inc. All rights reserved.

Trademark notice: Product or corporate names may be trademarks or registered trademarks, and are used only for identification and explanation without intent to infringe.

British Library Cataloguing-in-Publication Data
A catalogue record for this book is available from the British Library

ISBN: 978-0-367-50897-5 (hbk)
ISBN: 978-0-367-50898-2 (pbk)
ISBN: 978-1-003-05170-1 (ebk)

DOI: 10.4324/9781003051701

Typeset in Bembo
by KnowledgeWorks Global Ltd.

Contents

1	"Teachers are to DIIE for!": Why lesson planning is crucial and a question of competence and attitude	1
2	Diagnosis and discovery	19
	2.1 Analysis of the learner and the framework conditions	21
	2.2 Analysis of the lesson content	37
	2.3 Analysis of teacher professionalism	42
3	Intervention	54
	3.1 Goal planning	61
	3.2 Content planning	74
	3.3 Method planning	80
	3.4 Media planning	90
	3.5 Space planning	96
	3.6 Time planning	102
4	Implementation	108
5	Evaluation	117
6	Visible teaching: Know thy impact!	133
Appendix		*142*
References		*152*
Index		*156*

CHAPTER 1

"Teachers are to DIIE for!"
Why lesson planning is crucial and a question of competence and attitude

Some often-heard statements: "Beginners have to plan lessons. I now have enough experience." "Lesson planning – that's something for theorists. Practitioners do, and don't, talk about it too much." "Why should I plan a lesson? I've taught it so many times, I know exactly what I have to do."

Have you come across these statements before? In this chapter we want to discuss these views and examine them critically and constructively.

The aims of this chapter
Once you have read and worked on this chapter, you should …

Surface level: Know that
- Visible Learning is one of the biggest syntheses of meta-analyses of empirical educational research.
- teacher professionalism is a symbiosis of competence and attitude.
- lesson planning works better with a model than without a model.
- an integrative approach includes important elements for lesson planning.

Deep level: Understand how
- evidence is important in the discussion about learning success.
- teacher professionalism is manifested in the interaction of competence and attitude.
- lesson planning is based on evidence.

The success criteria of this chapter
In order to be able to achieve the stated goals, it is necessary to understand the following content:

1. Visible Learning as the foundation of empirical research in the classroom
2. Teacher professionalism as a symbiosis of competence and attitude
3. Selected results of empirical research on lesson planning
4. An integrative approach as a planning model

DOI: 10.4324/9781003051701-1

In March 2015 I was a guest at the International German School in Brussels. After a very stimulating and very pleasant experience of training, I had some time before my plane went back to Munich. I decided to drive downtown for a bit, watch people and enjoy the spring sun. I sat on a bench in front of the opera house. It didn't take long for three teenagers to get my attention and I made the following observation that still captivates me today: these three teenagers, I estimated them to be 13 to 15 years old, tried to imitate Taylor Swift's dance moves, which she showcased in her video "Shake It Off." It was impressive to see how the three teenagers pushed themselves, how they repeatedly tried to make progress in the song, how intensively they swapped ideas, showed, imitated, corrected one another, saw mistakes as opportunities and – last but not least – how much joy they had. Learning was visible in these moments. The time flew by. An hour passed and I had to make my way to the airport while the three teenagers continued to practice. I asked myself: Why can't school be like this?

We finished our book *10 Mindframes for Visible Learning* with the above observation (cf. Hattie & Zierer, 2024). In the present book, this conclusion is the beginning of our discussion. The crucial aspect of this observation was not what the three teenagers did. Much more impressive was how and why they did what they did. This is one of the central key messages from Visible Learning: success is not only based on knowledge and ability, not just on what people do but also on the attitudes, that is, the will and judgment, reasoning power, and zest for action. How people think about what they do, and what reasons they have for this, opens up scope for action. Without wanting to deny the importance of the competencies, without the appropriate attitudes success can often remain hidden or is brought to light only to a very limited extent.

If one transfers this idea to the work of teachers, one cannot avoid focusing on their core business: teaching as a largely planned, intentional, institutional, and above all educational activity. Successful teaching is not just a question of competence, not just a question of technology, not just a question of any method, but also a question of attitude. We would like to explain this throughout the book.

Since the results from Visible Learning above all are the basis for our ideas, we would like to present them first.

Visible Learning: the empirical foundation for this book

Research starts with a study, often published in a journal or in a thesis. Research syntheses or literature reviews then find many of these studies and make interpretative comments, suggest directions for new research, and aim to influence how we see schools and classrooms. Meta-analyses take these many studies and convert the main impact measure into a standardized measure (effect size), allowing reviewers to ask about the overall effect and any moderators (such as age, ability, socio-economic status) that may impact the overall effect.

In the Visible Learning research, over 2,300 of these meta-analyses have now been synthesized to ask about the relative effects of many influences (learners, home, parents, school, principal, teacher, strategies) and investigate the moderators. The MetaX website (www.visiblelearningmetax.com) includes the latest compendium of meta-analyses, and the many books by the two of us (and with colleagues) discuss the meaning of these effects. Collecting the meta-analyses was not the main work, but interpreting the meaning underlying the many meta-analyses is the biggest challenge of the discovery, and it is ongoing.

A major value of meta-analysis is the relativity of effects, although care is needed to interpret them. Indeed, it is detecting common themes among those effects that are higher compared to those lower than the overall average that has led to the development of the Visible Learning messages.

The work on Visible Learning spans over three decades. It began with the collection of data from meta-analyses in 1990, leading to the publication of *Visible Learning* in 2008. This work included over 800 meta-analyses and more than 50,000 primary studies, with an estimated 200 million learners participating (the estimate is due to the fact that the number of students is often not specified in the meta-analyses). At the time, it was one of the largest datasets of empirical pedagogical research ever evaluated. This was followed by *Visible Learning for Teachers* in 2013, which incorporated over 900 meta-analyses based on more than 60,000 primary studies. In 2019, *Visible Learning Insights* was published, drawing on over 1,400 meta-analyses and more than 80,000 primary studies, encompassing the performance results of an estimated 300 million learners. The most recent release, *Visible Learning: The Sequel*, published in 2023, includes over 2,300 meta-analyses and more than 130,000 primary studies, involving an estimated 400 million learners. For the latest information regarding the dataset, refer to the aforementioned MetaX.

	Visible Learning (2009)	*Visible Learning for Teachers* (2013)	*Visible Learning Insights* (2019)	*Visible Learning: The Sequel* (2023)
Number of meta-analyses	816	931	1,412	2,313
Number of primary studies	52,469	60,167	82,955	132,389
Number of students	approx. 200 million	approx. 240 million	approx. 300 million	approx. 400 million

To derive the general Visible Learning messages from the numerous primary studies, the primary studies must first be made comparable at the level of a meta-analysis. The statistical measure of the effect size is used for this – most often abbreviated as d. The calculation of an effect size presupposes that there either is a comparison between a pre- and post-measure following from some intervention (such as introducing a new method of lesson planning) or a comparison between some teachers who use this new method and some who do not. In Visible Learning the outcome is always defined as school learning performance, usually measured in terms of mathematical, scientific, and linguistic competencies (indeed, across most school subjects). Generally, a measure leads to an increase in learning performance if the value is positive, or it leads to a reduction in learning performance if the value is negative. If one takes this simple classification, a first look at the data from Visible Learning is interesting (cf. Hattie, 2023).

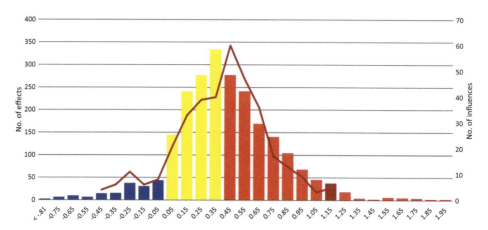

Figure 1.1 Distribution of the number of effects and summary effects.

Figure 1.1 shows that over 95 percent (yellow and red bars) of all influences and effects (y-axis: left / right: number of effects / influences) that have been empirically investigated lead to positive effects (x-axis: $d>0$). In this respect, almost everything that happens in the lesson promotes academic achievement. That could reassure us as teachers, but it shouldn't. To put it more critically, maybe it can be concluded that learning cannot be prevented.

This is particularly important for the topic of the present book. Because of this result, almost every teacher can claim that they have a positive impact on their learners – regardless of whether they plan lessons or not! Similarly, almost every teacher can claim that they can provide "evidence" of the success of their lesson. Claiming effectiveness, however, is trivial in the school context. Therefore, we oppose this interpretation and propose to set the zero point differently and shift it, namely to 0.4. Why 0.4? This value represents the average of all effect sizes of the dataset and marks the range of the "desired effects." The aspiration we are pursuing is simple but, we believe, convincing: to be better than average!

But we need to be very careful about using the overall average, in the same way that care is needed to talk about lessons for 5-year-olds, or for 10-year-olds – as the variability among 5-year-olds and among 10-year-olds can be enormous. There is a flaw in the average as the variability must also be considered. Further, if the outcome of a study is narrow, such as vocabulary words, then the chances of having higher impact (higher effect sizes) is much more probable than if the outcome is wide, such as creativity.

The effect size of 0.40 is useful for discriminating between all the effects in Visible Learning but may not translate without thinking into classrooms. Nevertheless, one implication is exciting and cause for celebration. There are many teachers, many programs, many schools that can gain >0.40 in learning, and the expertise to systematically make such gains is a hallmark of the profession and most worthy of celebration. Schools and teachers can add significant and most worthwhile improvements to student learning – and can do so regularly.

This shift from the zero point to the overall average of 0.40 is supported when one considers that individuals make learning progress through aging alone. We get smarter, even if we never go to school, simply by experiencing more dilemmas, problems, and people. These are called "development effects" and have effect strengths between 0 and 0.20. When we look at the effects relating to the typical teacher, these effects range between 0 and 0.40, which is why these values may be described as normal "school attendance effects." Any effects above 0.40 are deemed desirable – but we still have to be careful with these descriptors. Small effects can sometimes lead to important questions that help us understand why they are low and then know how to improve them (e.g., asking why the effects of class size are so low), and sometimes big effects could be on very narrow measures (e.g., increasing vocabulary scores). Negative values, which can be particularly problematic but rarely occur, are defined as "inverse effects."

The results of the synthesis of meta-analyses of more than 350 factors take into account virtually all aspects that influence school learning performance. They are assigned to nine different domains for better orientation, based on a classification scheme derived from the didactic triangle: "Students," "Home," "School," "Classroom," "Curricula," "Teaching strategies," "Implementation," "Learning strategies," and finally "Teacher" (cf. Hattie & Zierer, 2019).

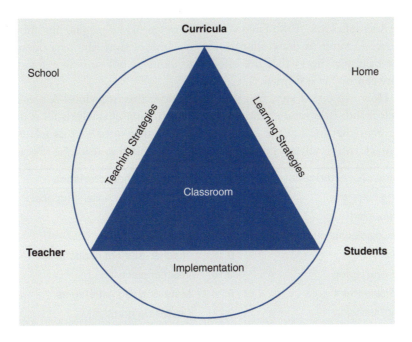

Figure 1.2 Domains of Visible Learning.

Any number of factors could be considered in order to show the importance of the domains and factors for the pedagogical success of children and adolescents. In this connection, we recommend referring to previous publications on Visible Learning. At this point, we will instead limit ourselves to the core message, which can be derived from the following selection of factors (cf. www.visiblelearningmetax.com/).

Factor	Effect size
Reducing class size	0.17
Ability grouping	0.21
Appropriately challenging goals	0.60
Open vs. traditional classrooms	0.02
Feedback	0.51
Finances	0.19
One-on-one laptop	0.16
Use of PowerPoint	0.26
Teacher credibility	1.09
Teacher–student relationship	0.62
Co-/team teaching	0.21
Teacher clarity	0.85
Multi-grade/multi-age classes	–0.01
Meta-cognition strategies	0.52
Deliberate practice	0.49
Advance organizers	0.41

A simple look at the table shows the range of the results, but also that it is not a trivial matter to draw educational conclusions from the data obtained. Rather, the example shows that the effect size alone is not sufficient for distinguishing between myths and impact.

How can one draw a first conclusion from this overview? A breakdown of the factors into structural characteristics and teaching characteristics is helpful. If one takes a closer look at the overview, one sees that some factors relate to structural characteristics, whereas others should be described as teaching characteristics.

Structural characteristics	Effect size	Teaching characteristics	Effect size
Reducing class size	0.17	Appropriately challenging goals	0.60
Ability grouping	0.21	Feedback	0.63
Open vs. traditional classrooms	0.02	Teacher credibility	1.09
Finances	0.19	Teacher–student relationship	0.62
One-on-one laptop	0.16	Teacher clarity	0.85
Use of PowerPoint	0.26	Meta-cognition strategies	0.52
Co-/team teaching	0.21	Deliberate practice	0.49
Multi-grade/multi-age classes	–0.01	Advance organizers	0.41

Let us start with the structural characteristics, which are always worth arguing about and fighting for. But the results from Visible Learning also show that structural measures alone have the least effect. For example, if class size is reduced, this has little effect on the learning success of students (mainly because teachers do not seem to change their practice when class size is reduced). This does not mean it is not worth considering this expensive structural change, but the decisive factor is how the teacher deals with the reduced class size. The situation is similar with finances: as important as this is and as much as one must campaign for having more money available, the effectiveness of this factor can only be seen from the perspective of what the money is spent on.

And thus, on to the teaching characteristics: teachers play a key role when it comes to the school performance of learners. But this does not apply to all teachers. Visible Learning thus initiates a new discussion with regard to teachers: it is about expertise, as this is what underlies many of the effects above the average. An expert teacher is not necessarily someone who only has a high level of subject matter knowledge; they must also be able to enter into a dialogue and build a relationship with the learners. Teachers must be able to translate their knowledge into the language of students. Howard Gardner correspondingly speaks of the "Three Es": Excellence, Engagement, and Ethics. The interaction between these three factors distinguishes expertise. At its core, it is about the passion for learning, about classrooms that invite learners to come and get involved with investing in learning. It is expertise that is visible in the school context due to the fact that the teacher's actions are characterized by care, control, and clarity; that their lessons offer challenges and trigger fascination while listening to the opinions and learning strategies of students and leading them to deeper understanding. For example, it can be shown that expert teachers pose much more challenging tasks, which require the application of the acquired knowledge as well as its transfer to previously unknown situations, while non-experts often limit themselves to tasks in which learners merely have to reproduce what they have just learned. Expertise in this sense does not depend on the number of years in the teaching profession or on the amount of work. It is about knowing how to set challenging goals, understanding where learners start, and how to bridge the gap between where they start and where they want to go, namely the success criteria.

Teachers therefore play a certain role in the lesson, which we refer to as an activator, an evaluator, and a change agent. Activators have the goals of the lesson in mind, review and adapt their selected methods, and make an impact on the students. Facilitators, on the other hand, work with greater reluctance to adapt their chosen teaching methods, believe the students can facilitate their own learning, and therefore leave learning more to chance.

It is crucial for a teacher as an activator to adopt evidence-based practices. There are many forms of evidence, from rigorous research designs with experimental and control groups and reflexive introspection (observation of students, artifacts of their work) to a combination of both. Visible Learning argues more for the latter and considers evidence from multiple sources, with more emphasis on the valid interpretation of this evidence. Evidence can be from teacher observation, from student voice and work, and from empirical and published studies – and it is the triangulation, critique, and interpretation of these sources of evidence that matters when making judgments about what best to do next. The research in Visible Learning can be seen as probabilistic – and we want educators to choose the highest probable interventions, but what equally matters is the fidelity and impact when they use the method. "Know thy impact" thus becomes a key phrase and means that the teacher asks about the effect of their own actions on the learning lives of students and seeks empirical evidence for this impact: How many students have benefited from this impact, and what is the magnitude or extent of this impact?

Expertise as a symbiosis of competence and attitude

The emphasis on expertise means attending to the thinking and decision skills of teachers. This is why we have formulated "10 Mindframes for Visible Learning" (cf. Hattie & Zierer, 2024):

1. Successful teachers talk about learning, not about teaching, and start and end their pedagogical and didactic considerations with the learner and their learning successes and skills. They take into account the prior knowledge and experience of learners and design their teaching in such a way that, building on this, fits as closely as possible with advancing the learner's level of learning to the next level of success.
2. Successful teachers set challenges and do not make learning processes too easy or too difficult or too boring. The aim is to create an optimal fit between previous knowledge and raising achievement to the next level of requirements, making learning as challenging as possible for each student (the Goldilocks principle).
3. Successful teachers see learning as hard work and enable diverse, regular, and challenging phases of practice. Learning should not be exclusively transferred into the hands of the learners as they do not always know the next best learning steps.
4. Successful teachers see teaching as an interaction based on appreciation and expectations of the learner and the requirement to invest in building positive relationships. In every form of schooling, it is therefore important that teachers seek positive interactions and conversations with and between learners.
5. Successful teachers do not see teaching as a one-way street but as a dialogue. They make cooperative learning possible and know a variety of methods to use class discussions profitably, both so they can hear their impact and for students to hear others thinking aloud. An aim is for teachers to "hear" the learning (the barriers and enablers) of each and all the students.

6. Successful teachers inform learners and parents about the language of learning. Each teacher needs to be an expert in learning and teaching. This knowledge must be shared so that learners can benefit from it.
7. Successful teachers see themselves as agents of change and do not use methods for the sake of methods or because they "like them" but always against the background of maximizing the learning situation for each and every student. The principle applies that media and methods are used in such a way that they contribute optimally to the achievement of objectives.
8. Successful teachers give and demand feedback because feedback is not only an important instrument for them to learn about their impact on learning but also is a critical dimension of teaching. They give and receive feedback from the learners and reflect on it promptly in order to be able to adapt the lessons if necessary.
9. Successful teachers see student assessments as feedback for themselves and about themselves and always associate both learning success and errors in the learning process with their thinking and doing.
10. Successful teachers work together. They strive for a common vision of education, critique each other's interpretations, and see school and teaching quality as a collective task. The focus on what impact means and steps of implementation are defined together and questioned again and again. Many forms of evidence serve as a basis for these discussions.

These ten mindframes must not be considered as a kind of "catalogue," which can be worked through in sequence. Rather, it is a whole, more like a network of important ways of thinking about becoming and being a teacher.

A characteristic of networks in general is that they shine through strength and their weak points can be compensated for by the rest – and all of this with a minimalist material expense. The spider's web is an interesting example in this context. Researchers have recently discovered that these networks are among the strongest of all structures, so that today they often serve as the basis for artificially generated networks in all areas (Cranford et al., 2012). The strength of a spider's web depends on two factors. First, the nature of the threads. If the threads are stretchable and tear-resistant, a strong net is the result. Second, it depends on the structure of the network. Depending on the distribution and arrangement of the meshes and openings, a network can be more stable or more unstable. If both factors complement one another, their influences increase and also have a compensatory effect – this can be observed perfectly in spider's webs, which remain stable or return to stability even if the wind has torn a hole in them. This property of the web is vital for the spider: patching a hole costs less time and energy than building a new web.

If one transfers this model to the present book, then the above ten guiding principles describe the threads of the net: the more pronounced these are, the greater their influence is on teachers' thinking and actions. At the same time, they interact with each other. If this is a loose parallel existence, there is no coherence –

the attitudes would be more like a patchwork than a unit. However, if they are mutually supporting, the attitudes form a structure and thus a stable network. In Aristotelian terms, the whole is more than the sum of its parts.

As a result, each guiding principle is related to the others. Each principle results from the others. Each principle interacts with the others. Each principle is supported and strengthened by the others. The requirement is therefore not trifling: all principles must be taken into account! This also shows the necessary coherence in educational contexts.

It is essentially about logical, consistent, and coherent thinking and acting in situations of uncertainty, unpredictability, and noise. The ten guiding principles in this book are an expression of pedagogical professionalism, can be learned and taught, and are the focus of continual improvement.

Often the objection is raised that there is not strong evidence that planning lessons leads to greater learning success on the part of the students. Some of highest-impact teachers do not have written plans. But it is not the medium of the plan (written or otherwise) that is important but the presence of planning and a set of planned behaviors and methods that allow for adaptation during the lesson. The more that teachers have clarity and challenge with regard to their goals, the more likely their students are to succeed in learning. The better these goals fit and stretch the learners then the more likely they are to succeed (fit relating to being appropriately challenging considering the skills and dispositions students bring to the class). The more teachers succeed in reaching agreement on the goals with the learners, the more likely they are to be successful. This alone justifies the need for lesson planning and learning design. In short: going from "Visible Teaching" to "Visible Learning" is the aim of this book.

Better planning and designing with models

There are now more than 40 planning and designing models all over the world (cf. Zierer & Seel, 2012). Hence, the question arises: Do such planning and designing models bring something worthwhile?

Planning and designing models aim to provide theory-guided and evidence-based recommendations for action to enable the analysis and planning of instruction that is as educationally effective as possible. For this reason, they focus on those aspects of instruction that the authors deem particularly significant for students' learning gains, thereby reducing the complexity of instruction. The perspectives taken vary according to the authors' theoretical and methodological backgrounds, ranging from more theory-driven approaches (e.g., the Berliner model and the Hamburger model) to more action-oriented designs (e.g., ADDIE and 4C/ID). Although the research field is extensive given this diversity, Visible Learning includes the factor "Lesson design," which has a high effect size of 0.79 (cf. Hattie, 2023). The results indicate that the effectiveness of didactic models is independent of learners' age, subject taught, and even type of school (cf. Costa et al., 2022).

Despite the differences among planning and designing models in detail, a comparative view reveals commonalities that serve as recommendations for action (cf. Zierer & Seel, 2012):

- Consider the goal level when analyzing and planning instruction. Ensure clarity and transparency by differentiating the goals and making them visible to students.
- Examine the subject matter comprehensively to clarify the essential aspects of competence acquisition for learners from a disciplinary, pedagogical, and learning perspective.
- Align methodological and media decisions with the goals of instruction so that neither methods nor media become ends in themselves.
- Evaluate your goal, content, method, and media decisions both during the instruction (formative) and at the end of a teaching unit (summative). Draw conclusions for the following instructional steps.

A common misunderstanding in dealing with didactic models is to confuse them with dogmatism. No didactic model claims to always be implemented one-to-one. As recommendations for action, they allow for flexibility that can be used with pedagogical responsibility. Certainly, over the course of a teacher's biography, the perspective on didactic models will change repeatedly, making them an essential aspect of lifelong learning in the teaching profession.

Even though the connections between teaching and learning are not linear and there are uncertainties, from an empirical perspective, didactic models demonstrate high effectiveness, and there is no doubt that instruction is better analyzed and planned with a didactic model than without one. In this sense, the question of using didactic models not only addresses the competence of the teacher but also their attitude: the willingness and conviction to analyze and plan a lesson over and over again, even if one has already taught that lesson. Because not only are the students different each time but the teacher has also become a different person.

Now the question arises, what is "good" planning and designing and how can we make it visible? In different research this question was investigated and among other things the following experiment was conducted (Zierer et al., 2015): How do the planning and designing differ when teachers plan and design either with a model (e.g., ADDIE model) or without a model? The result from Visible Learning was clear: better planning and designing came from using a model.

There are three aspects that improve planning and designing when using a model:

Perspectivity: Planning and designing models help to move from what the teacher will do to what the student will learn, from tasks that involve the students to do things to tasks that invite students to progress in their learning, and they anticipate the various learning journeys students will make during the lesson.

Dimensionality: Planning and designing models help to focus not only on the methods – for many the measure of all things in lesson planning – but especially on the discovery of what students bring to the class (in terms of their prior knowledge and understanding), their dispositions and motivations, and the success criteria of the lesson.

Level of understanding: Planning and designing models help not only to focus superficially on the tasks but also to go into depth regarding the nature of learning and cognitive complexity of the lesson.

Even though there hasn't been much research on the effectiveness of planning and designing models to date, the few existing findings clearly indicate their benefits. Planning and designing models are particularly effective when they open up many perspectives, consider different dimensions, and take into account various levels of understanding. The crucial point from an empirical perspective follows here: there is a lot of evidence at the more concrete steps of planning and designing models. Today, we know how learning objectives must be formulated, how clarity in instruction is to be established, how teacher–student relationships are to be built, how instruction must be organized over time, which methods are best to use when, and much more. Planning and learning models thus provide the framework to be able to pose these important questions and the evidence helps to answer them. Therefore, the following is of no doubt: better planning and designing results from using models!

"Teachers are to DIIE for!": an integrative approach as a framework

The starting and end points of a successful lesson can be seen in a planning and designing model. To then implement these plans requires successful implementation of the plan. This idea can be summed up by a central formula from Visible Learning (Hattie & Zierer, 2024): "Teachers are to DIIE for!" DIIE stands for "Diagnosis," "Intervention," "Implementation," and "Evaluation" (cf. Hattie et al., 2020).

The DIIE model is a framework that provides a shared language of teaching and learning; it allows all of us to capitalize on collective teacher efficacy in all learning environments, with the belief that we have an impact on our students' learning and with evidence to support that belief. The four stages of the DIIE model (Diagnosis/Discovery, Intervention, Implementation, and Evaluation) provide guidance as we engage in turning good ideas into high-impact learning experiences that move student learning forward. They deal with perspectivity, dimensionality, and level of understanding in multiple ways.

Diagnosis and discovery: Think back to those first few weeks of school. They seem to fly by with culture-building activities, assemblies, protocol meetings, establishing routines and procedures, and so forth. In those weeks, how are

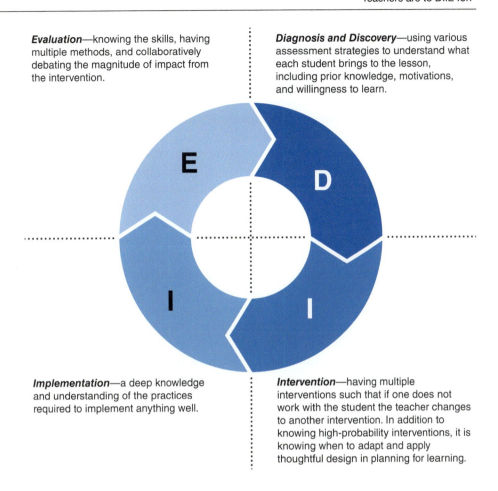

Figure 1.3 The DIIE model.

teachers taking time to learn about the dispositions that students bring into the class? It is so easy to get bogged down in the *what* of teaching, frantically planning lessons that link to essential curricular objectives and making sure we have our lesson plans in order. Evaluative thinking strategies challenge teachers to not think of the *what* but of the *why* and *who*. Our students are the most important determinants in our teaching. While many teachers spend their time figuring out what to teach, teachers who apply evaluative thinking skills are busy learning about who they will be teaching and what each student brings into the classroom or learning environment. The first component of evaluative thinking ensures that teachers are critically thinking about where their learners are in their learning journey and then where to go next in that journey. Where students are in their learning journey represents their learning capital and the place to start to develop our teaching potential. This is the focus of the diagnosis/discovery component of the DIIE model. When teachers take measures to determine what dispositions, unique characteristics, experiences, and learning opportunities students bring to the learning environment, their teaching practices have the potential to make a greater impact. Although the DIIE model uses the term "diagnosis" as a descriptor, it should be noted that we do not imply medical diagnoses. Instead, we suggest that teachers take measures to discover (diagnose) more about their learners before they attempt to teach content, skills, and understandings. For example, assume you were having a staff dinner party to celebrate the end of a school year. A logical step before cooking would be to ask the staff about any food-related allergies or dietary requirements. Discovering those will allow for a more personalized and inclusive menu for all diners, and will naturally lead to a better experience for all attendees. By using various assessment strategies to determine what students bring to class, we can be more impactful with our teaching to cater to the specific dispositions of our students.

Intervention: When teachers take appropriate measures to discover who their learners are, they can then move on to the second component of the DIIE model, intervention. Understanding the usefulness of interventions, when coupled with appropriate knowledge of who our students are as learners, is fundamental to ensuring maximum impact on student learning. When the first component in the DIIE model is overlooked, interventions may generate a positive response with students but still may not have the greatest impact. In other words, we do not maximize the potential we have with our learners. Because there are so many learning interventions available to us, it becomes increasingly difficult to sift through the list and determine which have the greatest potential to impact students' learning at this particular moment in their learning progression. Remember, almost everything works but your task is to identify what works best given the discovery of where the students currently are in their learning. We should be planning, designing, and implementing learning experiences based on the specific context of our learning environment and learners. This context absolutely includes whether we are in a face-to-face classroom or a remote learning environment. The planning must focus on the intentional selection of an intervention or approach to teaching and learning. Although the key to successful intervention lies in thorough discovery of student dispositions, unique characteristics, previous experiences, and learning opportunities, there is also a thoughtful process needed to incorporate specific interventions in your teaching and learning. Teachers must not only seek out high-impact approaches but should also understand there is a time and a place for using these approaches (cf. Hattie et al., 2020). In order to successfully select interventions, teachers should consider: Do we have multiple interventions available to us? (in case, with some students, the first does not work) Do we know when to apply these interventions? Do we know when to adapt or make changes to the intervention based on what we know about our learners?

Implementation: The third component of the DIIE model, implementation, is just as significant as having access to high-impact interventions. When we seek out evidence-based approaches to teaching and learning we can support our learners as they move forward in their learning journey – but only if we implement those approaches in an effective way. Due to the abundance of strategies and interventions available, we tend to experience information overload about which strategy or intervention to use and when. Think of a time a professional resource was passed along for your consideration and use by colleagues. Often these resources were recommended to you because one of your colleagues experienced some level of success in implementing this resource with their own learners. While it is fantastic that your colleague has found ways to implement this approach, strategy, or idea in a way that yields a positive impact on student learning, you must consider two things: (1) the local context of your own learning environment (face-to-face, hybrid, or virtual) and (2) the adaptations necessary to make this approach, strategy, or idea successful within your local context. The implementation process must ensure that evidence-based approaches (i.e., interventions) are clear to all stakeholders (e.g., students, teachers, parents) and vary in both applicability and task. These interventions would not only need to be identified but also implemented with fidelity to ensure our students make progress in their learning journey. Teachers should thus use a critical or evaluative lens when considering this stage. Implementation means knowing when to use certain interventions at certain times of the learning process.

Evaluation: We will never really be able to "know thy impact" on student learning without the evaluation of our practice. This must be done in collaboration with our colleagues or learners. The final component in the DIIE model, evaluation, tasks us with looking at the implementation of teaching strategies to determine the impact our decisions around interventions and implementation had on student growth and progress. As we evaluate our impact, we should note there is a distinct difference between student progress and student achievement. To truly implement teaching strategies equitably, students must be aware of their growth and progress, as well as the overall expectations of their learning outcomes (did they meet them or how close they are to the success criteria). These outcomes include academic, behavioral, and social-emotional outcomes. Successful evaluation of impact requires us to think back to the beginning of the DIIE model and really consider our initial decision making. While this may sound like a large philosophical consideration, we must keep the impact on our students' learning as the central focus. During the evaluation component of the DIIE model, we have to reflect on our previous decisions and determine where we are going next in our teaching and students' learning. As we reflect, we should know the expected impact of these learning experiences on our learners.

This once again highlights the symbiosis of competence and attitude that defines expertise. Against the background of the task of everyday lesson planning, a continuation of the ten principles explained above is necessary. When planning lessons, it is not just a question of competence and thus knowledge and ability. In this respect, although we present corresponding ability in the form of techniques, we will not offer a finished model in this book. Planning is always an attitude and, in addition to knowledge and ability, also requires willingness and values. In the ACAC model (cf. Hattie & Zierer, 2024) we have tried to illustrate this idea, and we will address this once again in detail below.

Figure 1.4 The ACAC model.

Successful lesson planning thus always comprises at least four major aspects: a comprehensive lesson planning phase including methods of teaching (intervention) based on a thorough analysis of the learning prerequisites (diagnosis and discovery), carrying it out in a high-quality manner (implementation), and evaluating it on the basis of evidence (evaluation). There is also attention needed as to the planning to know the significance of this analysis, planning, implementation, and evaluation in terms of their impact on the learning lives of students. In a nutshell: teachers are to DIIE for!

One of the greatest dilemmas in teacher education is that planning models often have a bad reputation with teachers – even though every teacher plans lessons according to a more or less elaborated model (written or mentally). In some instances, it is not possible to make the benefits of planning models visible for new teachers because the models are usually not articulated or written plans are not available from expert teachers. If the stakes are set too high – and teachers are compelled to execute to the detail the lesson plan – then no matter how small a mistake or deviation from the plan, this can be interpreted by the teacher educator or more senior staff as needing punishment, leading to a culture of error with negative connotations. Others may claim that "I do not need to plan or design learning; I have done it so many times before." Yes, but these teachers are unlikely to have experienced the learning and reactions to teaching for this particular cohort of students. Lesson planning and learning design is therefore necessary, as is the teaching of appropriate competence and an appropriate attitude in teacher training: Visible Teaching!

Exercises

Surface level

1. Sketch the key ideas of Visible Learning.
2. Create a concept map for your current planning activities. Please outline on one page what is important to you when planning a lesson and how you implement what is important to you. At the end of the book, we will ask you to revisit this reflection.

Deep level

3. Please evaluate the items listed in the following table relating to your ability, knowledge, will, and judgment and add up the points for the different categories (1 = strongly disagree; 2 = disagree; 3 = neutral; 4 = agree; 5 = strongly agree). Then enter the corresponding average values in the network diagram below. Following this, discuss the results with colleagues and think about the next steps to follow from this reflection.

Ability I am in an excellent position to ...	1 2 3 4 5
... analyze the starting point of learning.	
... carry out a comprehensive planning of lessons.	
... carry out the planning with high quality.	
... evaluate the implementation of the teaching based on evidence.	

Knowledge I know exactly ...	1 2 3 4 5
... what is important in the analysis of the learning situation.	
... what is important when planning the lesson.	
... what is important for the implementation of the lesson.	
... what is important when assessing the lesson.	

Will It is always my goal to ...	1 2 3 4 5
... analyze the learning situation.	
... plan the lessons comprehensively.	
... carry out the planning with high quality.	
... evaluate the lessons based on evidence.	

Visible Learning: Lesson Planning

Judgment I am firmly convinced that ...	1	2	3	4	5
... the analysis of the learning situation is decisive for learning success.					
... comprehensive planning of the lesson is crucial for learning success.					
... high-quality implementation of the planning is crucial for learning success.					
... an evidence-based evaluation of the implementation of the lesson is crucial for learning success.					

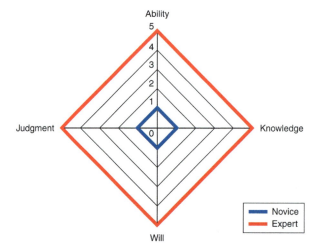

Figure 1.5

What are my next steps?

1. _____

2. _____

3. _____

CHAPTER 2

Diagnosis and discovery

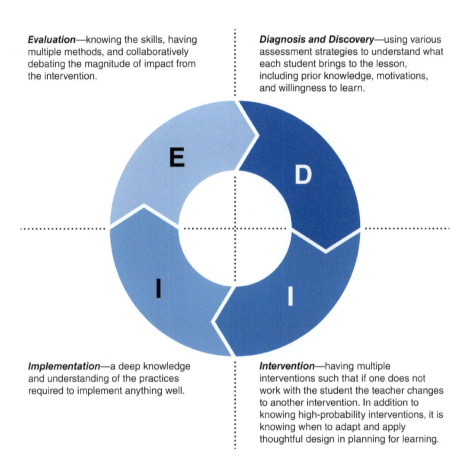

Figure 2.1

Evaluation—knowing the skills, having multiple methods, and collaboratively debating the magnitude of impact from the intervention.

Diagnosis and Discovery—using various assessment strategies to understand what each student brings to the lesson, including prior knowledge, motivations, and willingness to learn.

Implementation—a deep knowledge and understanding of the practices required to implement anything well.

Intervention—having multiple interventions such that if one does not work with the student the teacher changes to another intervention. In addition to knowing high-probability interventions, it is knowing when to adapt and apply thoughtful design in planning for learning.

The aims of this chapter
Once you have read and worked on this chapter, you should …

Surface level: Know that
- prior knowledge, learning behavior, social behavior, and working behavior are important on the part of learners in the context of the analysis of a teaching–learning situation.

DOI: 10.4324/9781003051701-2

- group development, group cohesion, and group composition within the classroom and family support among the home factors are significant in the context of the analysis of a teaching–learning situation.
- subject matter aspects, learning aspects, and educational aspects of the lesson content are significant in the context of analyzing a teaching–learning situation.
- competencies and attitudes associated with teacher professionalism and the school are important in the context of the analysis of a teaching–learning situation.

Deep level: Understand how

- aspects associated with the learners are more effective for learning success than other aspects.
- the extent to which the situational framework conditions in the class and in the parental home must be taken into account when planning lessons.
- to reflect on one's own competencies and attitudes regarding learning and teaching.
- to reflect on whether students' strengths and weaknesses can be seen with regard to the analysis of a teaching–learning situation.

The success criteria of this chapter

In order to be able to achieve the stated goals, it is necessary to understand the following content:

1. Analysis of learners and the situational framework: prior knowledge, learning, social and working behavior, and family support
2. Analysis of lesson content: subject matter analysis, learning analysis, and educational analysis
3. Analysis of teacher professionalism: competence and attitude

In this chapter, three major factors are considered during the diagnosis and discovery phase: the learner, the teacher, and the content. Students enter the class with varying skills, expectations, dispositions, and motivations. They bring situational factors such as recent experiences of bullying, home issues, interactions with friends, past experiences with the teacher, and their affinity or lack thereof for the subject, all of which contribute to their sense of belonging in the learning environment.

Teachers also bring their own beliefs about teaching and students, along with their lesson planning, expectations, depth of subject knowledge, and passion for imparting that knowledge. Additionally, subject matter knowledge, or the *what* of lesson planning and learner design, is crucial. This knowledge is influenced by factors such as the curriculum, the teacher's depth of content knowledge, and their methods of presentation.

Further, the division of the dataset from Visible Learning into nine domains – "Students," "Home," "School," "Classroom," "Curricula," "Teaching strategies," "Implementation," "Learning strategies," and finally "Teacher" – leads to three analyses:

In the first step, the analysis focuses on students and the situational framework. This primarily concerns factors closely related to the learner, which are found within the domains of "Students," "Home," and "Classroom."

In the second step, the analysis shifts to lesson content. Here, particular attention is given to factors within the "Curricula" domain.

In the third step, the analysis delves into teacher professionalism. This pertains primarily to factors within the "Teacher" domain, but also considers aspects from the "School" domain.

As a result, this chapter examines six of the nine domains in greater detail. The guiding question is which factors within these domains are significant for everyday lesson planning from an evidence-based perspective. The domains "Teaching strategies," "Implementation," and "Learning strategies," are not addressed in this chapter, as relevant factors within it become significant only during the concrete planning and implementation of teaching.

2.1 ANALYSIS OF THE LEARNER AND THE FRAMEWORK CONDITIONS

> Please answer the following questions for your class: Are there girls and boys in the class? Do the learners have parents of different socio-economic status? Do you have students who do not have a traditional family environment? Do you have learners with a migration background? Do students show differences in learning, working, or social behavior? Are there learners with a low or high motivation to learn and perform in their subjects? You can probably answer yes to any of these questions, which shows that heterogeneity in school and teaching is normal. In this chapter, we want to deal with this issue and consider, based on evidence, which aspects of heterogeneity should be taken into account in the context of lesson planning and which other aspects should also be considered.

We assume that you were presumably able to answer yes to all of the questions asked at the beginning of this section. Today, heterogeneity is normal in every class, in every school, and in every society. This normality is a challenge – above all because myths are often confused with truths in pedagogical policy discourses and also in scientific opinions. One of these myths is that every learner needs an individual learning path. If this statement is taken literally, the result in the described case would be that the teacher would have to organize 24 different learning arrangements – which no teacher can create and which is also not recommended in terms of the effectiveness of the learning arrangements. It is how teachers use group collaborative activities while attending to the learning plan of each student that is the skill. Against this background, we would like to present a number of empirical results, in particular to bring into the discussion those elements that we really know are effective. Lesson planning must focus on these aspects in order to be effective.

Analysis of the learner: taking a look at prior knowledge as well as learning and working behavior

First, let's look at the students. In the dataset of Visible Learning there are over 300 meta-analyses, including more than 25,000 primary studies and leading to over 70 factors. At least three key messages are important if we take a look at lesson planning:

First, certain factors mitigate against success in learning. These include, for example, "Maltreated children" (−0.63), "Boredom" (−0.46), "Anxiety" (−0.40), and "Depression" (−0.30). Hardly anyone will seriously doubt the importance of these factors for educational success.

Second, some factors have little to no influence. These include, for example, "Gender (male − female)" (0.00), "Positive ethnicity self-identity" (0.17), "Lack of sleep" (0.02), and "Mindfulness" (0.26). Perhaps we should be concerned with these, such as improving the view of one's own ethnicity, and also aim to understand why these are so low (e.g., most students are not sleep deprived, but when those few are there may be more serious consequences).

Third, particular factors can accelerate learning in the most desired ways. These include, for example, "Positive self-concept" (0.51), "Self-control" (0.66), "Deep motivation and approach" (0.58), "Working memory strength" (0.64), "Concentration-Persistence-Engagement" (0.41), and "Self-efficacy" (0.64).

The key message here is that there are individual factors that can make the difference. Most of these can possibly be enhanced by the teacher, not necessarily by accommodating to each individual's profile but by allowing for these unique attributes as part of the whole picture of the class. When you consider the top influences, they almost always apply to all students regardless of what they bring into the classroom.

Yes, we must start with excellent diagnosis, which means in-depth knowledge about the students in the class – their prior learning, their physical and attitude dispositions, their motivations and willingness to invest in learning, and their expectations and skills in learning. These, however, are starting points; they are not edicts to tailor every lesson to each student – and if we did such tailoring, we would miss the opportunity of building the community of learners, which is so desired by employers today and probably will be more so tomorrow. Can they work in teams, can they translate and teach others, can they respect themselves as unique contributors and respect others for what they bring to the task and context, and do they have confidence in their ability to contribute and learn from others? This is hardly likely to happen when individual teaching is dominant.

This analysis of learners can be determined as an analysis of learning requirements. If one follows the factors presented and thus evidence-based teaching research, it is primarily the questions about prior knowledge, learning behavior, and working behavior that have to be considered:

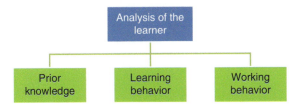

Figure 2.2

Connecting new learning to past learning is far more critical than connecting learning to real-world issues or the future aspirations of the student (or teacher). This is primarily because the student enters new learning with many ideas, many conceptions, sometimes misconceptions and misunderstandings, with motivations (or not) to invest to explore more new ideas – and without an understanding of this past learning it is all the more difficult to integrate new learning. For too many students, new learning is just more things to remember, not connected to what they already know or care about, and so it is no wonder they turn off, have negative attitudes, misbehave, or feel flummoxed.

There are many procedures for determining prior knowledge in more detail. In essence, they differ with regard to the degree of systematization and the depth of information. In this respect, they range from scientifically more robust tests to simple forms of questioning. First of all, in the area of prior knowledge, there are a variety of methods in the literature to determine prior knowledge in more detail. Basically, they differ with regard to the degree of systematization and the depth of information. In this respect, they range from scientifically sound tests to simple forms of questioning:

- Scientific tests
- Prior performance surveys
- Unresolved queries (e.g., acrostics)
- Asking questions

There are many forms of achievement tests, and the world is rapidly moving toward internet-based tests that can be adaptable, provide faster responses with reports and feedback, and make it easy to accumulate information about groups or the whole class or school (or system). An example is https://e-asttle.tki.org.nz

The e-asTTle tool, for example, provides a snapshot from a test about the strengths, gaps, achieved, and to be achieved aspects of the lesson. It can present information for each student, for the class, or for the school – helping students and teachers know what is already known, where to reteach, and where best to go next. It also, at the school level, can help leaders ascertain the optimal next

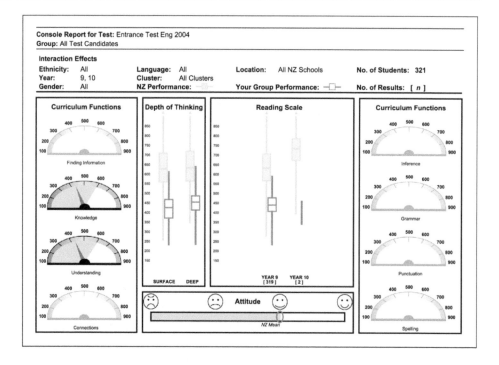

Figure 2.3

professional learning for teachers, while at the system level it can inform where to improve resources.

If no corresponding tests are available, then the teacher's own asessment methods can be used. In the core subjects of mathematics and language, these can be, for example, based on student work, a class test, or the last homework assignments. While not necessarily at the same high level of measurement robustness, this information is usually more honed to what the teacher is teaching right now. It helps teachers to identify strengths and weaknesses on the part of learners with regard to their prior abilities, their prior performance level, and perhaps their strategies and thinking about the work.

Even simpler and especially interesting is asking questions (factor "Questioning" with $d = 0.49$). When put in a meaningful way, they provide information on the previous knowledge of the students. An example in this context is acrostics, which are filled out in advance of the lesson and thus serve to help the teacher understand what knowledge and understanding the learners bring to the class, as well as helping the students make their own connections to past ideas and knowledge. For this purpose, the letters of the ABC are applied to the left side of a sheet, and the learners must then find a word for each letter that they already associate with the new topic. It is helpful not to stubbornly follow the ABC, but to jump to letters where an association is possible immediately. It can also be helpful to combine rare letters (e.g., X, Y, and Z) or to exclude letters from the ABC – until finally an acrostic is left, i.e., the letters of the new topic.

Finally, asking questions is a way of making the prior knowledge of students visible. Various questions are possible and can be differentiated with regard to the depth of knowledge. For example, it is worth querying the learning content from previous grades on the topic, which is mostly based on the curricular character of the lesson plans. Sometimes the following question is already sufficient: "What do you already know about the new topic?"

There are now a number of apps to aid in questioning that have the advantage that they can be used independently of time and space while at the same time alleviating teachers of time-consuming evaluation work. Social media aspects of the internet have proven to be especially valuable in enabling all students to ask and answer questions, when these same students are far more reluctant in class, in front of their peers, to ask or answer questions (Davies, 2016). Furthermore, from these internet-based questions, it is then easy to gain feedback, such as by using word clouds that can help make visible which associations learners have with a topic.

Part of the diagnosis before starting a lesson or series of lessons is understanding students' skills and confidence in working collaboratively with their peers. Unresolved queries and asking questions are particularly useful to get peers to talk to each other before the lesson. In view of the influence that peers and their interactions have on their learning progress in a subject, this difference should not be underestimated compared to more systematic procedures.

From this we can also identify groups of students who know more, some, or little about a learning topic. This can be the most important information to then decide on the pitch of the lesson, the right level of challenge, the ways to introduce new information connected to prior knowledge, and establishing a baseline to later assess the level of impact of the teaching on all the students.

Now to the areas of learning and working behavior, which are often viewed and assessed together. A variety of measures can be found in the literature. Of particular note are psychological tests, which were developed according to strict scientific criteria and can therefore measure learning and working behavior most precisely. But they are often psychiatric-medical tests and so are not suitable for the all-day analysis of learning and working behavior. For this task there are many freely available, worthwhile measures of some of the more important student factors, such as the above-mentioned factors "Achieving motivation and approach" ($d = 0.44$), "Deep motivation and approach" ($d = 0.58$), "Self-efficacy" ($d = 0.64$), "Positive self-concept" ($d = 0.51$), "Concentration-Persistence-Engagement" ($d = 0.41$), and "Working memory strength" ($d = 0.64$). The items in the following table could be used to begin to understand student skills in these domains (+ = strongly agree; 0 = neutral; – = strongly disagree):

Learning behavior: The learner …	+	0	–
Motivation			
… follows the lessons attentively.			
… puts their hand up regularly.			
… is enthusiastic about the lesson.			
… shows interest in the lesson.			
… asks questions about the lesson.			
Self-efficacy			
… prefers difficult tasks to easy tasks.			
… is able to work on tasks independently.			
… immediately asks for support when needed.			
… is able to solve tasks independently.			
… stays calm when there are difficulties.			

Working behavior: The learner …	+	0	–
Self-concept			
… uses mistakes made to continue learning			
… is discouraged by mistakes.			
… attributes learning success to his or her actions.			
… attributes learning success to lucky circumstance			
Concentration, persistence and engagement			
… is easily distracted.			
… remains focused.			
… works quickly.			
… works persistently.			
… works hard.			
… is able to do a lot of work over a longer period of time.			
Working memory			
… quickly remembers new content.			
… remembers details.			
… new knowledge will open up shortly.			
… remembers what has been learned for a long time.			

These items can be the basis for the analysis of individual students or groups of students. Essentially, they can be evaluated by learners and estimated by the teacher about a class of students. The core factor then is how to interpret and make decisions about the next actions – but at least these are more based on what the students bring to the class than based on nothing.

We do need care as, for example, consider the Dunning–Kruger effect. David Dunning and Justin Kruger (Kruger & Dunning, 1999) showed that weaker learners overestimate their abilities by up to 20 percent, whereas more powerful learners underestimate their abilities by up to 5 percent. They illustrated this effect by referring to McArthur Wheeler, who robbed banks while his face was covered with lemon juice. Wheeler believed this would make him invisible to the surveillance cameras, a mistaken belief based on his claims about the chemical properties of lemon juice as an invisible ink. In Dunning and Kruger's words (1999): "People tend to hold overly favorable views of their abilities in many social and intellectual domains … People who are unskilled in these domains suffer a dual burden: Not only do these people reach erroneous conclusions and make unfortunate choices, but their incompetence robs them of the metacognitive ability to realize it" (p. 1121). Harsh but worth contemplating. This does mean teachers are well advised to critically question below-average students' beliefs about their own learning.

It is important to understand the strategies students use in their learning. Too many use too few, often focusing on one major strategy – when it does not work the first time and they continue to use the same strategy, then no wonder some students believe they are poor learners. This focus on learning strategies is not in any way to be confused with the myths about learning styles (the belief that students learn better acoustically, visually, haptically, or communicatively). These methods have little evidence to support them. Similarly, we should not encourage students to ascribe to the myth that students retain 10 percent of what they read, 20 percent of what they hear, 30 percent of what they see, 50 percent of what they see and hear, 70 percent of what they recite, and 90 percent of what they do. At first glance, this may sound plausible, but at second glance it lacks any empirical evidence.

There is no support for the above claims, and too often these claims are used to justify why some students cannot learn, hence condemning them to the bottom of the distribution. Students need multiple strategies for learning; if they cannot process informationally then they need to be taught in multiple ways. However, we ask that they not be penned into a preferred style of learning. This search to identify the strategies and motivations of students should not be confused with learning styles.

Analysis of the framework conditions: classroom and parental home

In this section, the analysis of learners will be extended to include aspects that do not emanate from learners but are nevertheless directly related to them. This reflection is important for daily lesson planning and learning design because learning success can depend on what the student brings from the home, and how they react to the classroom dynamics. In Visible Learning there are factors that are particularly worth noting in the domains of "Classroom" and "Home."

Let us first look at the "classroom" as a whole. There are essentially three sets of factors with three key messages:

First, there are factors of very low impact. First and foremost in this context are "Modifying school calendars/timetables" ($d = 0.11$). The key message is to decide about these and move on to more important questions. They neither influence the quality of teaching nor is it worth considering these aspects in greater depth when planning lessons.

Second, certain factors can work when teachers bring them to life. These include "Reducing class size" ($d = 0.17$), "Open vs. traditional classrooms" ($d = 0.02$), "Multi-grade/multi-age classes" ($d = -0.01$), and "Ability grouping for gifted students" ($d = 0.21$). Overall, the effect has been (note the tense here) of limited impact and it is worth pausing to consider why. For example, class size reduction does enhance achievement (the effect is positive and not zero), but the size of the effect is far below what many initially would have thought (and many get upset it is so low as it defies their beliefs and expectations). The reason it is so low is that too many teachers do not change how they teach when moving from larger to smaller classes, so the key message could be to change how we teach to optimize the opportunities that fewer students provide (see Blatchford & Russell, 2020; Hattie, 2008). Similarly, open classes tend not to work when teachers use pot plants, bookcases, and filing cabinets to recreate their own classes, and do not truly team teach (and note the meta-studies are quite dated). More modern research shows remarkable impacts on learning when teachers collectively plan, teach, and evaluate together (Byers et al., 2018).

Third, there are factors that have high probabilities for working and must therefore be taken into account. The influences range from negative effects, such as the factors "Retention" ($d = -0.24$) and "Students feeling disliked" ($d = -0.26$), to positive effects, such as "Small group learning" ($d = 0.46$), "Enrichment programs" ($d = 0.49$), "Peer tutoring" ($d = 0.66$), "Decreasing disruptive behavior" ($d = 0.82$), and "Strong classroom cohesion" ($d = 0.66$). In this respect, these factors make it clear that interaction in the classroom is an aspect that requires special reflection in lesson planning.

For teachers, the following conclusions can be drawn: not everything that is visible as conditions in the classroom is important for learning success and therefore requires a systematic analysis. As teachers, we cannot (directly) influence many things that work or are harmful and yet are significant. It is good to know the circumstances for an understanding of the overall context without having to address them in detail in the planning. And finally, there are a number of factors that require special attention from teachers. They have to be placed at the center of the analysis of teaching and learning situations and thus at the center of lesson planning.

Against this background, the analysis of classes as a whole can be determined as an analysis of the group. If one follows the factors presented and thus of evidence-based teaching research and didactics, it is above all questions about group development, group cohesion, and group composition that have to be considered:

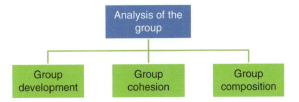

Figure 2.4

Below are a number of considerations that are not intended to be comprehensive. Rather, they follow the requirements of daily lesson planning, which must above all be efficient, and in this sense try to demonstrate the possibilities of analysis of classes as a whole.

First of all, in the area of group development. Generally speaking, there are five phases, which Bruce Tuckmann (1965) has formulated:

1. *Forming*: This phase is about getting to know a group. When children and young people enter a new class, many things are unclear to them. Teachers have a pivotal function in this phase because they can and must provide orientation. You have to take the lead. A group's high performance is not yet expected in this phase.
2. *Storming*: After making friends, all students know the teacher and one another. A role allocation consequently begins. As a rule, this does not occur without communication, and unfortunately sometimes not without power struggles. The latter can repeatedly disrupt lessons and therefore require sensitive chaperoning by the teacher. They have to act both as an arbitrator and as a driver. Group education processes and awareness of common successes are important impulses.
3. *Norming*: In this phase, a class has been found and the roles are allocated in such a way that working together is increasingly possible. Conflicts can arise repeatedly, but the group has already found procedures that help it solve these. Teachers increasingly intervene by moderating, advising, and monitoring compliance with rules in these procedures.
4. *Performing*: The better a group succeeds in developing a common vision, the more efficient it becomes. This phase is shown in classes in which students act increasingly independently and are given more and more tasks by the teacher – without overwhelming learners. A high sense of community and a high degree of team morality are characteristics.
5. *Adjourning*: This phase of group development describes the dissolution process and usually marks the "smelling the roses." The teacher's key task is to appreciate the common work with a look-back and to point out and prepare for further challenges with a look-ahead.

It should be noted that this group development can be seen as ideal, and in everyday life it is possible to go back and forth between the first four phases.

Any conflict situations can disturb everyday teaching and tie up a lot of time and energy. But the impact on learning of not developing a positive classroom culture can be serious: "Decreasing disruptive behavior" ($d = 0.82$) and "Classroom management" ($d = 0.43$) point to this.

It is not uncommon for social behavior to be either a hindrance or a driver for group development. Similar to the context of learning and working behavior, there are a number of procedures for evaluating social behavior, including psychological tests. Oriented observations and surveys are suitable for an everyday analysis of social behavior, which can be filled in by learners and by the teacher. The following table contains a number of sample items (+ = strongly agree; 0 = neutral; – = strongly disagree).

Social behavior: The learner …	+	0	–
Related to classmates			
… behaves fairly in the class.			
… gets along peacefully with their peers.			
… listens to others.			
… responds to the concerns of their classmates.			
… expresses themselves appropriately.			
… initiates group processes.			
… takes on tasks and duties.			
Related to conflicts			
… accepts other opinions.			
… resolves conflicts peacefully.			
… represents their own interests in the class.			
… urges compliance with agreed rules.			
Related to the teacher			
… listens to the teacher.			
… expresses their opinion appropriately.			
… follow the teacher's instructions.			
… is friendly.			
… is helpful.			

Making social behavior visible already provides clues for group cohesion. It is known from numerous studies that children with disruptive behavior have to struggle with "Students feeling disliked" – this factor ($d = -0.26$) has a remarkable negative effect. However, group dynamic processes remain hidden and can be viewed using other methods.

An effective tool for this purpose is sociograms, which were developed by Jacob Levy Moreno. They are now also available digitally (e.g., "Social Network Visualizer"), which means that they can be used efficiently. First, the teacher formulates questions that should make relationship structures visible in the class. For example, you can ask "Who is your best friend in the class?", "Who don't you know about?" (Friendship), "Who is the most popular child in the class?", "Who is the least popular child in the class?" (Popularity), "Who do you want to sit next to most?" and "Who do you not want to sit next to least of all?" (Collaboration). Then the relationship structures are illustrated with the help of a graphical preparation, mostly using arrow diagrams. In this way, the teacher can see a lot of information about a class and can see at a glance who is a friend or an outsider. For working in the class, especially when it comes to group formation, this information is just as important as the learner's level of performance. It is essential at this point to note that the sociogram contains sensitive data that should not be in the hands of the learner and should not be presented to their parents. It only serves to facilitate the analysis of the class by teachers.

An example for a sociogram is the following. The direction of the arrow shows the direction of the relationship. The box around the name is stronger the more often this learner has been named. The color green is used to make a seat neighbor wish visible and the color red for the opposite:

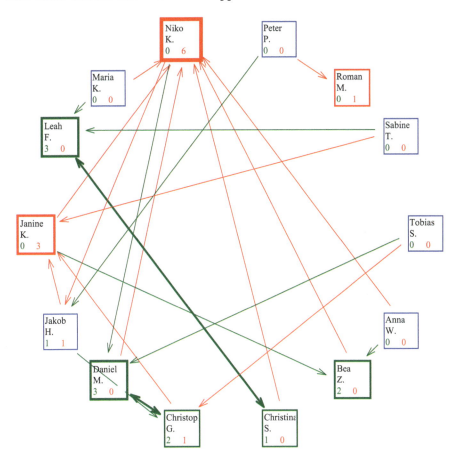

Figure 2.5

In this example, it becomes apparent that Janine K. and Niko K. are among the less popular learners, whereas Leah F. and Daniel M. are among the more popular children. Christina S. and Daniel M. are class leaders.

One step of the analysis of the class considers the group composition. The factors "Within-class grouping" ($d = 0.16$ and "Small group learning" ($d = 0.46$) indicate that merely focusing on grouping can lead to quite variable outcomes: If the group composition of aspects is determined such that the tasks they undertake in groups is not directly related to learning, this does not typically lead to any significant learning effects.

We also note Rob Coe et al.'s (2014) finding that 90 percent and over of students sit in groups and work alone in the UK. But students like the social interactions in groups, and one way to ensure the student-to-student interactions are positive for the whole class is to rotate the group membership at random from time to time. So, finally, an evidence-based answer can be given to the question of how large groups should be: no smaller than three and no larger than five learners form the optimum size (Swanson et al., 2017).

Now let us look at the family situation. Basically, two conclusions can be drawn from the data of Visible Learning:

First, the majority of factors are irrelevant to concrete lesson planning. This is mainly because they are beyond the influence of a teacher and are primarily the responsibility of parents. The main reason for this is that the effects associated with these factors cannot actually be effective – quite the contrary. However, teachers are powerless when faced with the question of whether a father or mother is unemployed or not (e.g., the factors "Family on welfare/state aid," $d = -0.12$; "Mother employment," $d = 0.05$), whether the child has a migration background or not (e.g., "Immigrant status," $d = 0.01$), whether the child is adopted or not (e.g., the factor "Adopted vs. non-adopted children," $d = 0.21$), or whether parents are in a stable marital relationship or not (e.g., the factor "Non- vs. divorced families," $d = 0.26$). Many of these questions are passionately discussed in public; however, as can be seen, the effects of these family factors are quite small but in some cases are important to the child.

Second, there are some critical family factors that can have major impacts on student learning. The level of parental expectations about learning and success for their children, and the level of parental support for learning ("Parental involvement," $d = 0.30$), are important. Parents with low expectations, who rarely support or talk about learning at home, can be a major delimitor ("Parental expectations," $d = 0.50$). Note, the key message is to talk about learning, not demand high grades or doing a student's homework for them. It is important to listen to their experiences of learning, helping them see errors and mistakes as opportunities for learning, and engaging them in worthwhile challenges. Both parents and their children should talk about the strategies and ways of learning while engaging in these challenges. It is about talking about learning, not merely valuing high grades, and certainly not merely about "what did you do today?" – in a lot of "doing this" and "doing that," there can be little learning. The effects of homework are fascinating – very low in elementary school and much higher in high school. Why? The major reason is that homework at any age is more powerful when it is an opportunity to practice something already taught (and this is the typical homework in high schools). There should never be a project or task that requires the parents to teach their children or, worse, do the task for the child. Parents can support the completion of homework, but the key message is to construct homework tasks that involve deliberate practice of something already taught.

It is so much more valuable for the child when the messages from the teacher and from the home are consistent – valuing learning, valuing errors and mistakes, valuing success and engagement in challenging tasks, valuing respect for self and respect for others, and building trust in teachers to do their job and parents to do theirs (together and separately). But in cases where this may not be happening in the home, the class must be a safe haven for students to develop these valuable attributes.

As teachers, an important key message must be formulated from what has been said: the family home has a decisive influence on the success of teaching. Of course, this cannot be influenced during a lesson and therefore eludes any need for planning. But the influences are so effective that it is important for teachers to take note of them and address them in the context of work with parents. For some of the influences of the family home support the results of empirical pedagogical research without question: pedagogical success only succeeds with parents and not without them. Therefore, teachers have to cooperate in different ways and try to get parents on board as partners. It is usually not a question of appointing them as auxiliary teachers – unfortunately, this is not infrequently the conclusion that is drawn in a misunderstood empiricism: parents spend hours and hours explaining to children what their homework is, where the challenges are in the tasks, and create one presentation after another. This has nothing to do with pedagogically meaningful work with parents, let alone with the effective involvement of all parents in school. On the contrary, if parent work is interpreted in this way, it leads to frustration on the part of the parents because overload can quickly occur and, in the worst case, a social disadvantage because parents from pedagogically poor milieus may struggle with these tasks, causing their children to fall behind. It makes learning more effective when you make parents aware of their role, how important they are in supporting their children, and what influence they have when they talk to and listen to them. In the early years, the power of language in the home is very high. Talking to children, listening to them talk, allowing them to ask *why* questions, and ensuring play activities are invested with language are critical for helping them to develop theories of their worlds, learn how to interact with others, and prepare for the next phase of literacy and oral development of language.

In our view, this is particularly the case in the study "The early catastrophe: 30-million-word gap" published by Betty Hart and Todd R. Risley (cf. Hattie & Zierer, 2024). Hart and Risley visited families for over two years in order to explore the interactions between children and their parents at home. Of interest was the connection between family interaction and the socio-economic status of the parental home. The knowledge gained is remarkable: children from an educated environment have almost three times as much vocabulary as children from an uneducated environment. This difference does not disappear in the following school years; there is a Matthew effect – the rich get richer, the poor stay poor (cf. Pfost et al., 2014). In this respect, there is no so-called wash-out effect, according to which school and teaching would end up compensating one another. On the contrary: the differences not only remain but even increase. One reason for these differences in language skills is the level of domestic stimulation with regard to linguistic engagement with the children. From their observations, Hart and Risley arrived at the following calculation: children from educated backgrounds hear up to 45 million words up to the age of four, whereas children from uneducated backgrounds only perceive 15 million words. This results in the trenchant "30-million-word gap." But the story is deeper than just these quantities, and there are also critical qualitative differences. Hart and Risley also examined what the relationship between language encouragement and language discouragement looks like, for example. Here, too, there is a clear result: children from educated environments receive encouragement up to seven times more often than discouragement, and children from uneducated environments hear discouragement more than twice as much as encouragement. So parents should talk to their children over and over again, listen to them, and encourage more talking and listening (cf. Hart & Risley, 2003).

Exchange these ideas with the parents again and again, and make them aware of their role. Involve parents in school and classroom situations, where they are capable and never where it is your responsibility. And record on your diagnostic questionnaires how you assess the influence of the parental home and what measures you have taken to improve parenting work at this point.

Exercises

Surface level

1. Reflect on the impact of the following factors on student achievement and decide what options you as a teacher have on the effects of these factors.

Factor	d: $<0, <.4$ or $>.4?$	Influenceable: yes or no?
Achieving motivation and approach		
ADHD treatment with drugs		
Anxiety		
Attitude towards content domains		

(Continued)

Diagnosis and discovery

Factor	d: <0, <.4 or >.4?	Influenceable: yes or no?
Autism		
Belonging		
Boredom		
Breastfeeding		
Concentration-Persistence-Engagement		
Creativity and achievement		
Cross-laterality		
Deep motivation and approach		
Depression		
Dialect use		
Emotional intelligence		
Field independence		
Gender (male–female)		
Illness		
Lack of sleep		
Maltreated children		
Mastery goals		
Mindfulness		
Morning vs. evening		
Performance goals		
Positive ethnicity self-identity		
Presence of mobile phones		
Pre-term/low birth weight vs. Full term		
Procrastination		
Relative age within a class		
Relaxation		
Self-efficacy		
Student personality		

Deep level

2. Discuss with colleagues learners' prior knowledge, as well as their learning, working, and social behavior and family support. Reflect on the possibilities and limits of the diagnosis of these factors in your class.

3. Survey with colleagues the learners' prior knowledge, as well as their learning, working, and social behavior, and discuss the result. To do this, either insert ticks in the following target diagram (maximum values toward the center) or fill in the following table (− = low, 0 = middle, + = high):

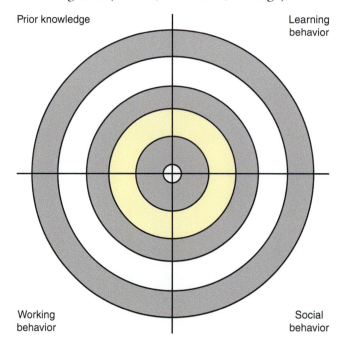

Figure 2.6

Name	Previous marks	Prior knowledge	Learning behavior	Working behavior	Social behavior	Family support

4. Use the data collected to fill in the following overview. Pay attention to brevity, simplicity, and conciseness to develop the necessary efficiency for everyday lesson planning.

Learner	
Learning behavior	
Strengths	Weaknesses
Working behavior	
Strengths	Weaknesses
Social behavior	
Strengths	Weaknesses
Family support	
Strengths	Weaknesses

2.2 ANALYSIS OF THE LESSON CONTENT

Please answer the following questions about the lesson content: Why is the lesson content imperative for these students' education? Could the lesson content be replaced by another topic? Are there reasons why your students should learn this? Are there steps that can be identified that must be understood in order? What are the relations you want the students to make between the ideas in the lesson? What is a context that would show they can transfer what they learn to a new context? Do learners need to adapt their language and complexity in order to understand it?

Answering these questions shows that analyzing the content of the lesson is a challenging task. In this section, we will look at this issue and consider, on an evidence-based basis, how the analysis of lesson content can take place in the context of everyday lesson planning and what criteria can be used to do so.

Answering the questions asked at the start of this section, we would like to look at the Visible Learning dataset. The domain "Curricula" is important now. There are essentially three key messages: first, it is striking that no factor from the

"Curricula" area has a negative effect. No matter which program is implemented, students take something from it. This underpins our pointed emphasis (Hattie & Zierer, 2024) that just aiming for increasing achievement is not good enough. This is reassuring on the one hand but not very helpful on the other. Second, it becomes apparent that the subject matter perspective is moving to the fore. As we will discover, it is both an appreciation of the content and the depth of relations between ideas within the subject that matter most. Third, factors with high levels of effect (e.g., "Science programs," $d = 0.50$; "Mathematics curricula & programs," $d = 0.38$; "Comprehensive reading programs," $d = 0.57$) suggest that a subject matter perspective alone is not sufficient. Successful curricula always include examples of ways in which the lesson content can be conveyed, what to look for when learning the lesson content, where there are pitfalls of understanding, and so on.

The following conclusion can be drawn: the analysis of lesson content always includes a subject matter analysis, a learning analysis, and an educational analysis. The focus of a subject matter analysis is on the correct presentation of the facts that are based on the state of the subject matter knowledge and the deeper conceptual relations between the various parts of the subject matter. In contrast, an educational analysis draws attention to the importance of the lesson content for the life of the students. Finally, a learning analysis focuses on learning in order to identify the key steps of understanding and explaining from the point of view of the students.

Figure 2.7

Subject matter analysis of lesson content

A subject matter analysis is the basis, on the one hand, for crystallizing the educational content of the lesson and, on the other hand, enables the most important learning steps in the learning analysis to be identified. In this respect, the evidence shows the effectiveness of the factors "Clear goal intentions" ($d = 0.44$), "Goal commitment" ($d = 0.44$), "Appropriately challenging goals" ($d = 0.60$), and "Success criteria" ($d = 0.66$). We need to be sure what the goals of the learning and lessons are, as well as communicating these goals clearly to the students.

Hence, there is a need to investigate the topic thoroughly, identifying the major learning intentions and the nature of the success criteria. A plethora of resources can now be accessed (e.g., on the internet) that allow you to quickly learn the major ideas and deeper conceptual thinking relevant to the particular lesson. If supporting material is available, for example from a textbook, this also can offer an initial and basic subject matter analysis. There is also much value in exchanging ideas with colleagues and, above all, seeking a conversation with any available specialist group (in school, across schools, or online, as well as contacting academics, as many are keen to advance their passions). Finally, take a blank sheet of paper or use a digital tool to write down the key points for developing the learning intentions, success criteria, and content (the big ideas and the main conceptual understandings) of the lesson. "Concept mapping" ($d = 0.62$) is recommended as a way to bring an overview to this planning.

Educational analysis of lesson content

Educational analysis in lesson preparation involves integrating learning requirements with subject matter analysis. If this dual process – combining content decisions with learning analysis – is not effectively managed, students may acquire some knowledge but still lack deep understanding.

1. When learning primarily concentrates on subject content knowledge, education rarely then challenges or improves thinking, doing, or feeling.
2. When learning is primarily aimed at cognitive aspects of individuals, it can fail to help students comprehend the *why* of the learning or its relations to other domains, or how to transfer knowledge to build more of a whole-person experience with learning. Howard Gardner (2013) has formulated this idea most clearly with his theory of multiple intelligences: besides cognitive intelligence, individuals also have emotional, aesthetic, spiritual, and many more intelligences. No intelligence exists without the other, as they interact with one another.
3. While in principle everything can be learned, educators select content based on normative reasons. Much of what can be learned is not educationally effective. One simply doesn't need to know it and therefore doesn't need to learn it.

The outlined juxtaposition of learning and education is not intended to open up contradictions but rather to clarify dependencies. Therefore, the learning content must be distinguished from the subject matter content. This then makes the motivation and engagement factors as important as the content to be understood from the lesson. The aim is to move from motivating students to merely learn the content ("Surface motivation and approach," $d = 0.00$) to a deeper appreciation of the content ("Deep motivation and approach," $d = 0.58$), or an appropriately more strategic approach to master both the surface content and deeper learning aspect of the lesson ("Achieving motivation and approach," $d = 0.62$).

When it comes to everyday lesson planning, two levels of reflection hold significance for pedagogical analysis. First, the legal frameworks of schooling, typically enshrined in constitutions, delineate a broad understanding of education. Second, curricula underscore and interconnect the educational significance of individual subjects. These two layers of reflection interact, laying the groundwork for the elaboration of teaching objectives.

Learning analysis of lesson content

The starting point in the lesson is connecting to what students already know and understand (and sometimes to what they misunderstand). Connecting to prior knowledge ("Prior achievement," $d = 0.73$; "Prior ability & intelligence," $d = 0.96$) and the ways of thinking ("Piagetian levels," $d = 1.28$) are critical as these prior notions provide the "coat hanger" that the students often use to incorporate and interpret new ideas. Primarily, the qualitative methods outlined, including ABC lists and question formulation, offer significant insights. Notably, close attention must be given to everyday conceptions, often misconstrued as precepts but more accurately termed pseudo-concepts. Recognizing this as educators is essential for effectively integrating scientifically validated concepts into pedagogical practice.

An important tool for conducting learning analyses is the SOLO taxonomy ("Structure of Observed Learning Outcomes"), developed by John Biggs and Kevin Collis in 1982. The SOLO taxonomy is famous for categorizing learning outcomes, but it is also useful for categorizing levels of understanding. It consists of five levels: At the prestructural level, learners have no understanding of the task or concept. As learners move to the unistructural level, they grasp one aspect of the task or concept. In the multistructural stage, learners understand several relevant aspects but may not integrate them into a coherent whole. As learners progress to the relational level, they can relate different aspects of the task or concept and understand how they are interconnected. Finally, at the extended abstract level, learners can generalize their understanding and apply it to new situations or contexts.

In learning analyses of learning content, teachers can use the SOLO taxonomy to design learning activities, assess student understanding, and provide feedback. This emphasizes the progression of learning from basic comprehension to deeper, more complex understanding.

Another tool to gradually make the learning process more challenging is didactic reduction. This is an educational concept aimed at simplifying complex content or topics to a more accessible and understandable level. In this process, unnecessary details and complexities are removed to facilitate learners' entry into a topic and enable better comprehension. This reduction can occur in various ways:

1. Content reduction: Only the most important and fundamental information is presented to promote understanding. Complex details are initially omitted and gradually introduced as the learner becomes ready.
2. Linguistic reduction: Complex technical terms and linguistic constructions are avoided or replaced with simpler and more easily understandable expressions. This allows learners to focus on the essentials without being distracted by unnecessarily complicated language structures.
3. Structural reduction: Information is transformed into clear and well-structured formats such as diagrams, tables, or charts. This facilitates understanding by visually representing complex relationships.
4. Temporal reduction: Complex processes or sequences are reduced to their essential steps to facilitate better understanding. This can be achieved through the use of time-lapse representations or summaries.

Didactic reduction aims to make the learning process more effective by reducing barriers to understanding and helping learners focus on the essentials. The prerequisites for didactic reduction are, first, that the subject matter remains academically correct; second, that there is academic compatibility with subsequent lessons; and third, that there is a fit with the students' ability levels. Therefore, didactic reduction is not about simplification through reduction but about providing challenge through an appropriate learning analysis.

Exercises

Surface level

1. Name the three areas of lesson content analysis and two factors that underpin their consideration.

Deep level

2. Explain *why* the analysis of lesson content includes the areas of subject matter analysis, learning analysis, and educational analysis.
3. Develop with colleagues an analysis of lesson content and discuss the result. Use the following figure as a "placemat." After intensive discussion in the first step, the second step is intended to bring the points raised in the discussion together. Everyone has to work on the field (e.g., "learning analysis") in front of them for a certain time window (e.g., 20 minutes) and then turn the "placemat." Hence, there is a new field into which a colleague has already written. In this respect, in the third step, the task is to complete their reflections, so that, after a further turn, all fields of the "placemat" are filled in.

Visible Learning: Lesson Planning

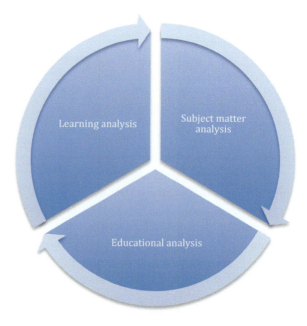

Figure 2.8

4. Use the data collected to fill in the following overview. Pay attention to brevity and succinctness in order to develop the necessary efficiency for routine lesson planning.

Lesson content
Subject matter analysis: What is the key idea of the content?
Educational analysis: What is the educational benefit to the content?
Learning analysis: What are the essential steps for surface and deep understanding?

2.3 ANALYSIS OF TEACHER PROFESSIONALISM

Please answer the following questions: How important is it to you that every child in your class achieves the best possible learning progress? What does a year of learning mean to you? How important is the exchange of ideas in your school about questions of teaching quality? How often do you plan lessons with other colleagues?

How do you deal with the mistakes around you – and all of us – every day in class? In this section, we want to deal with these issues and consider, based on evidence, which aspects of teacher professionalism have to be taken into account in the context of the teaching planning and which aspects have to be considered beyond that.

You've probably found yourself pondering over the introductory questions. Maybe you've even entered a defensive mode: "Given the current structures, none of this is possible," "It would be nice to plan lessons together, but it doesn't work," and "We all make mistakes – but everyone makes their own." These are just a few possible responses we're outlining, but we don't want to challenge these responses – they are important and reflect a state of mind. Rather, our goal is for teachers to make these states of mind the subject of their thinking. Ultimately, this results in a framework of thought, which we will later describe as attitudes, that influences what we do. Therefore, it's the question of how we think about what we do, and why we do something, that can particularly stimulate the professionalization process of teachers. We will also address the fact that group exchange is most effective for this purpose. Consequently, our aim in this section is not to tell you how to think about what you do. Our goal is to prompt you to reflect on what you do, and especially to use evidence-based criteria as a basis for reflection.

Therefore, let's look at the domain "Teacher." In the dataset of Visible Learning there are over 80 meta-analyses, including more than 4,000 primary studies and leading to over 20 factors. At least three key messages are important if we take a look at lesson planning.

First, there are a number of factors that seem to have no effect on learning success yet are often passionately discussed (e.g., the factor "Teacher performance pay," $d = 0.05$). Second, there are factors that constantly appear in discussions and are almost mythically debated (e.g., the factor "Teacher personality," $d = 0.27$). Third, there is a set of factors relating to teachers' expertise that counts. This can be seen, for example, in "Teacher expectations" ($d = 0.58$), "Teacher–student relationships" ($d = 0.62$), and "Teacher credibility" ($d = 1.09$). One factor seems to be surprising: "Teacher subject matter knowledge," with an effect size of $d = 0.13$. How can it be, even though 90 to 95 percent of teacher education focuses on this? In *10 Mindframes for Visible Learning*, we considered the following interpretation at the beginning of the book, which we will repeat briefly at this point:

Everyone knows teachers who know a lot but are not able to pass on their knowledge. They lack didactic competence – in other words, the skills to present content in a clear way, to be able to explain facts well, to be able to show essential knowledge and, even more specifically, be able to create a clear and helpful worksheet. Likewise, everyone knows teachers who know a lot but are so unapproachable that they cannot relate to learners. They lack pedagogical competence, in other words the skills to establish contact with students, as well as to create an atmosphere of security, trust, and confidence. Professional competence on its own therefore does not lead to an increase in school performance. In addition, teachers must have pedagogical and didactic competence (cf. Hattie & Zierer, 2024, p. 24f.).

A balance of both – teacher subject matter knowledge and the skills to teach – is needed so that students learn the content and then move more deeply to relating to, extending, and transferring this content. If only surface content is seen as valued in a class, then the level of teacher subject matter content does not matter. It is the linking of professional competence with pedagogical and didactic competence that is important. In this triad, expertise certainly occupies a prominent position – but only in this triad. Taken on its own and isolated from other areas of competence, expertise cannot be effective. Thus, we do not need less competence. Likewise, we must not dismiss the areas of competence as irrelevant. Rather, it is necessary to have a high level of expertise and to combine this with an equally high level of pedagogical and didactic competence.

The payoff and thus the most important result from Visible Learning now follows: even a high degree of professional competence, pedagogical competence, and didactic competence is not enough to teach successfully. In other words, knowledge and ability are not enough to be a successful teacher. The different types of competence should be linked and related. In essence, therefore, this concerns the question of what understanding of their role teachers have, what they understand by learning and what by teaching. So how do teachers think about what they do? An example: a teacher may have the opinion that mistakes are something to be avoided (students certainly feel this way about errors). The consequence is obvious: learners will learn from this teacher that it is better not to make a mistake. As a consequence, a fear of errors is created. How different is the interaction in the classroom when the teacher considers mistakes necessary for learning success – because mistakes make learning visible, because mistakes show what learners can achieve, because mistakes make it clear where to set the challenge, because mistakes open up the chance to maintain positive relationships, because mistakes make feedback all the more worthwhile, and so on. A lesson that sees mistakes as something to avoid stifles creativity and innovation in the bud. In this respect, certain areas of inquiry are opened up, which can be summarized under the term "Attitudes."

First, against the background of Ken Wilber's (2001) epistemology, competence can be defined as the field that focuses on knowledge and ability. In contrast, attitudes relate to will and judgment. Specifically: when people do something, they access competence in the form of knowledge and ability. Underlying this action are attitudes in the form of will and judgment. People always have certain reasons for doing something (or not doing it), which result in motivations and ultimately lead to a retrieval of knowledge and ability.

Second, following Jürgen Habermas' communication theory (1995), the reasons that guide people can be located in at least three worlds: a subjective world, an objective world, and a social world. If one transfers these reasons to the concept of attitudes, it becomes clear that attitudes are a collective term for three starting points of motives. First, starting from a subjective world, desires and interests can be the basis for actions. Since these factors only essentially apply to the individual, it is convictions that guide action. Second, starting from an objective world, empirically provable facts and proofs are the basis for actions. These have a general claim to validity and can therefore be described as settings. Third, starting from a social world, values and norms, rules, and rituals play an important role when it comes to motivations. Since these are not determined by the individual and are not obtained by empirical measurement, they are in the core evaluations that are conducive to action. Consequently, attitudes encompass not only approaches but also judgments and beliefs. Each of these areas is effective and significant, although attitudes form the approach that has the closest connection to empirical pedagogical research.

Thus, it can be stated that knowledge and ability in the subject, didactics, and education prove insufficient for possessing pedagogical expertise. Further, the attempt to base professionalism in the teaching profession primarily on knowledge and ability is reductionist and necessarily runs the risk of neither meeting the human nor the pedagogical challenge of teaching and learning. Pedagogical expertise — the term is used to overcome the historically charged discourse on the right understanding of teacher professionalism — is thus not only evident in knowledge and ability but above all in will and judgment. These considerations lead to the conclusion that in pedagogical contexts it is not only important what (knowledge and ability) teachers do but it is at least as important how (will) and why (judgment) they do something. In the ACAC model that we introduced in Chapter 1, we have tried to illustrate this idea.

Before drawing conclusions for the teacher from what has been said and transferring results to daily lesson planning, it is worth taking a look at the domain "School." This is because there is a factor that confirms a basic idea, which has already been formulated: the factor "Collective teacher efficacy" with an effect size of $d = 1.34$. What does the "Collective teacher efficacy" look like? In essence, this factor emphasizes how important it is within a school to collectively discuss questions of the impact of school and teaching quality. Successful schools are characterized by having collectively defined for themselves what their vision of school is and what good teaching looks like for them. In this respect, it is not enough for a college to formulate and display a mission statement. Rather, it is about living this mission statement on a daily basis, underpinning it with data, and working continually on its refinement. It's obvious that this can't just be about talking about schools and teaching. Simply exchanging materials is also inadequate. Instead, the discourse about what teachers do is crucial.

The factor "Collective teacher efficacy" thus shows how important it is that colleagues not only exchange ideas about what they are doing but also ask how and why they do what they do, and discuss together what they mean by impact and efficacy (e.g., clarify the following questions: What is the learning progress over a year in relation to learning effort? Who is making this progress and who is not? And what does this mean for pedagogical processes?). It is therefore a matter of making the reasons for one's own thinking visible to colleagues, agreeing on a common goal, and living, examining, and further developing this common cosmos of values every day, in every lesson, in every teacher–student conversation (cf. Hattie & Zierer, 2019).

As teachers, the following conclusions have to be drawn from the domains of "Teacher" and "School": not everything one can discuss passionately is a key consideration in the context of lesson planning. Instead, it pays to focus on two areas: first, on the development of teacher professionalism as a symbiosis of competence and attitude; second, on forms of cooperation and collective efficacy. If in the future we manage to talk more about the impact of teaching (and less about the structures), then we can all improve schools and teaching sustainably. Lesson planning offers the central field of action.

Figure 2.9

In the following, proposals are made for how both of the above areas can be developed in an evidence-based manner and how they can be (further) developed for everyday teaching planning.

First of all, we will focus on attitudes. In Chapter 1 we have already formulated guidelines, which we pick up in the table below. Please take these principles and reflect for yourself on the extent to which you agree with them and how you are already able to implement them. This reveals a gap that must be overcome in the course of professionalization: the gap between thinking and action. The following table may be helpful.

Please estimate your own expertise, ticking your responses with two colors: **How much do you agree with this statement (blue) and how well are you able to implement this statement (green)?**	**1 2 3 4 5**
Successful teachers talk about learning, not about teaching, and end their pedagogical and didactic considerations with a focus on learners. They take into account learners' prior knowledge and previous experiences, designing their lessons in such a way that aligns with these factors to result in the greatest possible fit, building on the learning status of learners.	

(Continued)

Please estimate your own expertise, ticking your responses with two colors: How much do you agree with this statement (blue) and how well are you able to implement this statement (green)?	1	2	3	4	5
Successful teachers set challenges and shape learning processes that are neither too easy nor too difficult or boring. The goal is to create an optimal fit between prior knowledge and learning goals, making learning as challenging as possible.					
Successful teachers help students see learning as hard work and enable diverse, regular, and challenging phases of work. Teaching should open up opportunities for students to learn deliberately.					
Successful teachers see teaching as an interaction based on trust and thus invest in building positive relationships. It is therefore also important that teachers engage in positive interactions and conversations with learners, who spend a large part of their time in school.					
Successful teachers see teaching not as a one-way street but as a dialogue. They enable cooperative learning and know a variety of methods to use class discussions profitably.					
Successful teachers inform learners and parents about the language of learning. Every teacher is an expert of learning and teaching. This knowledge must be shared, so that learners can also benefit from it.					
Successful teachers see themselves as change agents and use methods not for the sake of the methods but always against the background of the learning situation. The principle applies that media and methods must be used in such a way that they contribute optimally to the achievement of goals.					
Successful teachers give and request feedback because feedback is not only an important instrument for them but a critical dimension of teaching. They give and receive feedback from learners and reflect on this in a timely manner, in order to be able to adapt lessons if necessary.					
Successful teachers see student performance as feedback for themselves, always using both learning success and mistakes in the learning process to reflect on their own thinking and doing.					
Successful teachers work together. They strive for a common vision of education, viewing school and teaching quality as a collective task. The steps of the implementation are defined together and questioned again and again. All forms of evidence serve as a basis for discussion.					

The so-called SWOT model (Humphrey, 2005) is suitable for further work with this reflection. The acronym stands for the words "Strengths," "Weaknesses," "Opportunities," and "Threats." In a general form, the following representation is often used:

SWOT analysis	
Strengths	**Weaknesses**
Where are my strengths? What can I still build on?	Where are my development fields? What must I improve?
Opportunities	**Threats**
What I am using too little? What can I build up?	What must I avoid? Where are they lurking?

Now take your answers to the expertise questionnaire and consider where your strengths, weaknesses, opportunities, and threats are. Then enter it in a SWOT model and consider which changes you would like to initiate and which development tasks you would like to undertake. The following strategies can be helpful for this:

Strategy	
Extending	Using existing resources in connection with existing opportunities
Making up ground	Deriving opportunities from existing difficulties
Securing	Using strengths to counter risks
Avoiding	Preventing the concurrence of difficulties and risks

In the following, we provide some thoughts on teamwork. Unfortunately, teachers are often socialized as loners and many prefer to invest in solo teaching with the doors to their classrooms firmly closed; they prefer to plan alone, write their own exams, and grade alone. This aloneness begins from day one: every career-beginner stands alone in front of the class. If we now add the competition for permanent employment places, it becomes apparent that in teacher education fighting as a lone wolf can be widespread. In view of this socialization on the one hand and the effectiveness of the collective on the other hand, the implementation of a team structure is one of the biggest challenges in schools. In this respect, it is important to take into account attitudes on the one hand and competencies with a view to cooperation on the other.

The following gradation is helpful and should be borne in mind. It tries to make visible that cooperation must be learned and will not succeed immediately.

Steps of cooperation
1. Getting into a conversation with one another.
2. Supporting and criticizing one another.
3. Planning and assessing lessons together.
4. Teaching a lesson together.

At this point we would like to counter the objection that is repeatedly formulated: "Why should I cooperate? I can do everything better and, above all, faster myself." Matt Ridley formulated the following example to refute these and similar statements (Ridley, 2010; cf. Hattie & Zierer, 2024):

> Adam and Oz can make both spears and axes. While Adam takes four hours to make a spear and three hours to make an axe, Oz takes one hour to make a spear and two hours to make an axe. If there is a need for both of them to make a spear and an axe, it takes Adam seven hours and Oz only three hours.

	Adam	Oz
Spear	4	1
Axe	3	2
Total	7	3

Now what happens if they work together? At first glance, collaboration will be of little use to Oz because he will hardly save himself time if he goes ahead and makes a spear and an axe with Adam at the same time. But what if both do the following: Oz uses his strength and produces two spears in two hours; in return, Adam uses his strength and produces two axes in six hours. Both then make a trade and each of them has a spear and an axe. Adam, like Oz, thus had to invest an hour less in order to get a spear and an axe.

	Adam	Oz
2 spears	0	2
2 axes	6	0
	Trade of spear and axe	
Total	6	2

Without a doubt, trade and cooperation lead to a gain in time for both sides – we neglect the fact that it is quite possible to make a spear or an axe to a better or worse standard. If humans alone can use this temporal gain, it is already a form of collective intelligence. This gain becomes all the more manifold the more complex the tasks to be mastered.

Please now replace the spear with designing a lesson and the axe with a school assignment. Then think further: please replace the spear and the axe with ideas for teaching, experiences with regard to the evaluation of lessons, feedback, goal formulation, teacher–student relationship, motivation, exercise, differentiation, class leadership, and so on. In view of these considerations, collective intelligence no longer only becomes apparent in terms of a gain in time but above all in the power of the dialogue-based process, in the power of exchange and cooperation, and in the professional further development of the team. All this is more than merely an exchange of information and materials, merely a collection, merely a filing. Collective intelligence becomes visible in intensive, critical, constructive, and concentrated discussions about one's own competencies and attitudes.

Finally, the factors of "Teacher and teacher training" and "Micro-teaching" will be discussed in more detail, as this will provide important indicators for the further development of the teacher's professionalism in general and teaching planning in particular. With both factors, it becomes clear that a focus on certain questions, joint planning, execution and evaluation, intensive and regular exchange among colleagues, critical and constructive handling of mistakes, application of teaching videos and lessons, as well as comprehensive feedback (especially at the level of self-regulation and thus the next steps) are guarantors of success. In this sense, successful teacher training as well as successful micro-teaching focus not only on the competencies of teachers but also on their attitudes.

It is time for us to develop a culture of exchange and cooperation in schools in order to be able to use collective intelligence for the benefit of learners and also for the benefit of teachers.

Exercises

Surface level

1. Outline your understanding of teacher professionalism, taking into account the distinction between competence and attitude.

Deep level

2. Take the printed questionnaire provided earlier in this section on self-assessment of teacher professionalism and fill it in. Then complete the following SWOT analysis.

SWOT analysis	
Strengths	**Weaknesses**
Where are my strengths? What can I build on?	Where are my development fields? What must I improve?
Opportunities	**Threats**
What am I still using too little? What can I develop?	What do I have to avoid? Where are they lurking?

3. Record a lesson on video. Analyze it either by placing ticks in the following target diagram (maximum values at the center of the diagram). Alternatively, please complete the following questionnaires (either by ticking or with the help of a digital tool), which we will discuss in detail in the chapter on the evaluation of the teaching–learning situation. Fill in the ellipsis in the diagram

with another point that is of special interest for you. Afterwards, you will discuss your observations and conclusions with a colleague (who you can of course invite to come to the lessons themselves and then also ask to fill in the questionnaires). The goal of the exchange is to make the strengths and weaknesses of your professionalization visible.

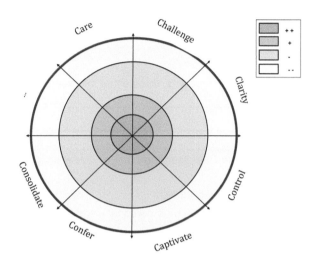

Figure 2.10

1 = disagree; 2 = tend not to agree; 3 = tend to agree; 4 = agree

Care	1 2 3 4
The teacher greeted students in a kindly and appreciative manner.	
The teacher provided an anxiety-free atmosphere.	
The teacher was interested in whether students really learned anything.	

Challenge	1 2 3 4
The tasks in class were challenging for students.	
The teacher had high expectations of students.	

Clarity	1 2 3 4
In the classroom a clear red thread was recognizable.	
The teacher showed students what the content of the lessons was related to.	
The teacher showed students what they need the new content for.	
As a rule, the teacher has built on content that students already knew.	

Control			**1 2 3 4**
In the classroom, clear rules, which the teacher specified, were recognizable.			
The teacher wasted no time through delays or idling.			
The teacher provided a trouble-free working atmosphere.			
The teacher had a good overview of what was happening in the class.			
In the classroom, clear rules were recognizable, which the teacher specified.			
In the case of violations by students, the teacher intervened quickly and consistently.			

Captivate			**1 2 3 4**
The content of the lessons was taught by the teacher in an interesting way.			
The course of the lessons was varied.			
Students were able to determine their personal learning progress through the lessons.			
The requirement level in the lessons was appropriate for students.			
The pace of learning in the lessons was appropriate for students.			
Students were able to apply strategies in the classroom, which are also useful for other topics.			

Confer			**1 2 3 4**
The teacher judged student performances fairly.			
The teacher gave helpful feedback on student performance.			
The teacher was fair and unbiased toward students.			
The teacher gave students meaningful feedback on their contributions.			

Consolidate			**1 2 3 4**
In the classroom, learning and exercise phases alternated.			
The teacher showed in the lessons exactly how students can solve certain tasks.			
Students had enough time to deal intensively with the content of the lessons.			
In the classroom there were ample opportunities to practice the new content.			

Diagnosis and discovery

What are my strengths and what are my weaknesses?

1. _____

2. _____

3. _____

4. Use the data collected to fill in the following overview. Pay attention to brevity, simplicity, and conciseness in order to develop the necessary efficiency for everyday lesson planning.

Teacher

Ability: in the subject? in education? in learning?

Knowledge: in the subject? in education? in learning?

Will: in the subject? in education? in learning?

Judgment: in the subject? in education? in learning?

My strengths

My weaknesses

CHAPTER 3

Intervention

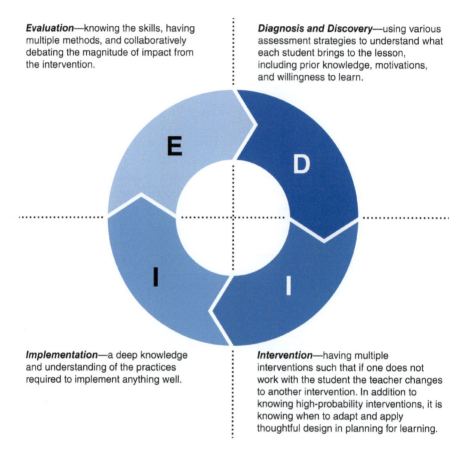

Figure 3.1

The aims of this chapter

Once you have read and worked on this chapter, you should …

Surface level: Know

- which aspects are important when planning a teaching–learning situation.
- which aspects are important with regard to goal decisions when planning a teaching–learning situation.

- which aspects are important with regard to content decisions when planning a teaching–learning situation.
- which aspects are important with regard to method decisions when planning a teaching–learning situation.
- which aspects are important with regard to media decisions when planning a teaching–learning situation.
- which aspects are important with regard to content decisions when planning a teaching–learning situation.
- which aspects are important with regard to decisions regarding rooms/spaces when planning a teaching–learning situation.
- which aspects are important with regard to time decisions when planning a teaching–learning situation.

Deep level: Understand how
- goals, content, methods, media, space, and time have to be considered when planning a teaching–learning situation.
- goals, content, methods, media, space, and time decisions depend on each other.
- to give reasons why the quality of instruction needs to be a guiding factor, especially when it comes to methods and media decisions.
- to convert the goals, content, methods, media, room, and time decisions into a planning script
- to reflect on whether your strengths and weaknesses can be seen with regard to the planning of a teaching–learning situation.

The success criteria of this chapter

In order to be able to achieve the stated goals, it is necessary to understand the following content:

1. Goal planning
2. Content planning
3. Method planning
4. Media planning
5. Space planning
6. Time planning

In this chapter, the aspects that are worth noting in the context of everyday lesson planning are examined in more detail based on evidence-based criteria. A selection of significant criteria is presented, for which, first, there is empirical evidence of their efficacy and, second, which form the basis for successful lesson planning.

The following note is essential: the *planning* of the teaching–learning situation follows an *analysis* of the teaching–learning situation. Accordingly, the analytical steps, as explained in the previous chapter, form the basis for this chapter, which is essentially about converting the results of the analysis obtained into planning steps.

Since six of the nine domains have already been examined in more detail in the previous chapter, the missing three domains, "Teaching strategies," "Implementation," and "Learning strategies," follow in this chapter. They contain several factors that are important for the concrete planning of the lessons. Since the domains "Teaching strategies," "Implementation," and "Learning strategies" themselves contain around 120 factors, it will be necessary to focus on everyday lesson planning in a way that does not focus on research details but rather on the core teaching practice messages that take center stage. This is an important and necessary focus, especially for beginners. To achieve this, the following steps are taken in the discussion:

In the first step, preliminary considerations are made, which is necessary due to the number of factors mentioned in these domains. In this respect, to derive key messages and recommendations for action, the domains "Teaching strategies," "Implementation," and "Learning strategies" are examined in more detail. The results obtained will be used to address models of teaching quality. It will become clear that although these are targeted and heuristic research summaries, they do not offer the potential to function as working models. They are too abstract and too theoretical to allow this transfer. As a result, a change of perspective to specific teaching planning is introduced by explaining the most important planning considerations alongside the didactic decision fields of goals, content, methods, media, space, and time. The didactic hexagon thus obtained functions as a working model and also as a further structural tool for the present chapter.

In the second step, success criteria are explained. The starting point is that teachers emphasize the importance of goals for the success of teaching, and that analysis of what learners bring to the lesson, in particular their prior knowledge, is a critical determiner in these success criteria.

In the third step, the decision field of content is examined. It will be necessary to address the analysis of lesson content. Based on this, it is clarified how tasks must be formulated and designed.

In the fourth step, the decision field of methods is considered, which is the most comprehensive concerning the number of factors. It is not uncommon to have debates about certain methods being more effective than others. However, it is often forgotten that it is not the case that the method works by itself. Rather, consideration should be given to the quality of implementation, the appropriateness and alignment of the teaching method with the nature of the content and success criteria, and the evidence that the method chosen is leading to the impact desired – efficiently and effectively.

The fifth step is to focus on the decision-making field of media. The debate about the research results makes clear that of greater importance than the technology itself is how this technology is integrated into the teaching process. In this respect, in this section, procedures are explained to be able to answer the question of media use in an evidence-based manner – it is not technology that decides why, how, and what is learned, but rather the quality of teaching using technology (or not).

In the sixth step, the decision field of teaching space is explored. Questions regarding space are often associated with questions of learning. The fact that teaching space – as well as all other factors – depends on qualitative considerations is emphasized in this point. In this respect, the analysis of learners and the resulting prior knowledge, learning, working, as well as social behavior play an essential role in answering evidence-based questions of seating arrangement and classroom design.

And in the seventh step, the decision field of time is subjected to more detailed consideration. Planning always leads to the question of the efficiency of time, so that under this perspective the other decision-making fields can, indeed must, be merged.

Let us begin with the domain "Teaching strategies." The current Visible Learning dataset covers over 200 meta-analyses with more than 20,000 primary studies. Out of over 40 influences five key messages can be drawn.

1. It is obvious that no single factor has a negative effect. Against this background, the recurring discussion about identifying the best method is understandable because they all work from an empirical point of view! In this respect, the frequently asked question "What works?" is misleading. To put it crudely, the only thing that students need in order for them to learn is a pulse. Only when the heart stops beating will nothing be learned.
2. A number of factors that deal with the area of the following goals show above-average efficacy: "Advance organizers" ($d = 0.41$), "Goal commitment" ($d = 0.44$), "Clear goal intentions" ($d = 0.44$), and "Appropriately challenging goals" ($d = 0.60$) all have effect sizes beyond the tipping point and thus greater than 0.4.
3. In the domain of "Teaching strategies," there are factors that emphasize the dialogue-based process of teaching in a special way ("Questioning," $d = 0.49$; "Peer tutoring," $d = 0.66$; and "Classroom discussions," $d = 0.82$). In this respect, successful teaching must always be conceived as a dialogue, not a monologue, involving all participants.
4. There are procedures that demonstrate the visualization of learning content ("Worked examples," $d = 0.47$) as well as methods for illustrating the learning process ("Concept mapping," $d = 0.62$).
5. The factors "Feedback" ($d = 0.51$), "Planning and prediction" ($d = 0.83$), and "Response to intervention" ($d = 0.73$) point to the significance of excellent diagnosis and teaching–learning strategies. Due to its efficacy, a separate chapter is dedicated to this last feature.

Before any conclusions are drawn for everyday lesson planning, the first step is to look at the other two domains. The domain "Learning strategies" covers over 200 meta-analyses with more than 15,000 primary studies. Essentially, the key messages drawn from over 40 factors confirm the key messages from the domain "Teaching strategies."

1. All factors in this domain have an effect size greater than 0.00. Thus, the vast majority of teachers can claim to be successful in teaching. But it's about more than just teaching successfully – because as argued above this is trivial. It is about supporting learners in the *best* possible way.
2. The bundle of factors that transfers the majority of responsibility to learners in the learning process is interesting: for example, "Student control over learning" ($d = 0.02$) and "Individual instruction" ($d = 0.24$). All of them only result in effects of less than 0.4. Thus, to rely on learners' own responsibility may create great expectations from a pedagogical point of view but, unfortunately, they cannot be substantiated empirically. Novices do not know what they do not know; hence students need expertise, and here the teacher is critical to provide guidance as to optimal success criteria, teaching methods, feedback, and much more.
3. There is a set of factors that conveys and focuses on certain learning strategies. Most influences achieve effects greater than 0.4: "Imagery" ($d = 0.55$), "Underlining and highlighting" ($d = 0.42$), and "Outlining and summarizing" ($d = 0.62$). Learners may not have optimal learning strategies or necessarily know when to use them; they may have to be taught these strategies and when to use them. However, if learners have learned these strategies, then these strategies are among the most powerful factors for learning success. And ultimately, these strategies are also core to assisting learners to take more personal responsibility in their learning. Thus, to get back to the point: learners must be supported, so that they can learn to become their own teachers – and above all want to do so. Successful learning is a question of competence and attitude.
4. Successful learning always depends on offering learners the right method at the right time. There is no method that is the best for all learners at any moment of the learning process. The choice of method must always be linked to the analysis of learners, the analysis of learning materials, the place in the learning cycle moving from surface to deep to transfer, and the analysis of teacher professionalism. In this respect, differentiation is the consequence.
5. The factors "Spaced vs. mass practice" ($d = 0.59$), "Deliberate practice" ($d = 0.49$), and "Practice testing" ($d = 0.49$) show the importance of reflection and consolidation in learning and within the lesson design. Students need to be taught, and time in the lesson created to learn how to practice regularly, and variously. Understanding the learning process thus becomes an important teaching principle and at the same time becomes an important source of information for all questions regarding the evaluation of teaching.
6. The factor "Time on task," with an effect size of 0.46, indicates that successful learning processes require a time structure. COVID-19 highlighted the importance of efficiency in teaching and learning, and this is an important message. And finally, three factors make you listen: "Perceived task value"

($d = 0.46$), "Self-verbalization/self-questioning" ($d = 0.58$), and "Strategy to integrate with prior knowledge" ($d = 0.93$) land well above the tipping point of 0.40 with their effect sizes.

Finally, the domain "Implementation" covers over 150 meta-analyses with more than 9,000 primary studies. In addition to the key messages formulated above, there are four more with regard to the factors of the domain "Implementation."

1. The bundle of factors for cooperative learning ("Cooperative learning," $d = 0.53$; "Cooperative vs. competitive learning," $d = 0.58$, and "Cooperative vs. individualistic learning," $d = 0.62$) and "Jigsaw method" ($d = 1.20$) clearly shows that learning takes place optimally in dialogue and that peers can be powerfully involved in the learning process. In spite of the necessity of individualization, learning is so often a social process.
2. The research shows that cooperation in class does not work on its own. Each of us knows group lessons that are boring and ineffective. It is not uncommon to observe that the learners sit in groups but work alone. As effective as cooperation can be in class, it is not a sure-fire success but requires preparation, like the factors "Direct instruction" ($d = 0.56$) and "Scaffolding and situated learning" ($d = 0.52$).
3. The bundle of factors on the use and effectiveness of digital media indicates that they certainly have potential to achieve greater learning success. But they also show that this is all the more the case when the use of digital media is preceded by thorough professional, pedagogical, and didactic reflections. Consequently, technology is not used for its own sake but assumes a supportive function, especially in fostering dialogue, and the social media functions of media can be used to create opportunities for students to think aloud when working with peers and teachers.
4. The factor "Problem-based learning," with an effect size of 0.45, underpins the already-mentioned necessity to pick up on the analysis of the learning requirements and to differentiate them in the classroom. If it is used at the right time it can achieve effect sizes above 0.4 (especially for high-performing learners); if it is used at the wrong time it can also result in negative effects (especially for low-performing learners). The same can be said for the factor "Homework" ($d = 0.29$), which when implemented correctly (providing opportunities to deliberately practice something already taught) can be highly effective and is therefore essential for sustainable learning success. Consequently, once again, it should be noted that it is not the method itself that always works to the same extent everywhere. The quality of lesson design is crucial.

The attempt to derive key messages from the domains "Teaching strategies," "Learning strategies," and "Implementation" shows how learning can be successful. This question has always been of concern to empirical pedagogical research and has often been translated into a number of models of teaching quality. The more well known include the so-called "7 C's of Effective Teaching" of

MET projects (2010) (Control, Clarify, Challenge, Captivate, Care, Confer, Consolidate) or the three basic dimensions of teaching (efficient class management, classroom climate, and cognitive activation, cf. Klieme, 2018). Likewise, the key messages formulated are reflected in the well-known criteria categorizations by Jere Brophy (1999), Hilbert Meyer (2004), and Andreas Helmke (2014). As different as these models appear at first glance, there are common themes: the similarities are greater than the differences. It does not matter which model is ultimately followed in lesson planning; it is more important that a model or a synthesis of different models is the basis of the planning. This ensures that empirical results provide the framework for lesson planning.

It is crucial that the models are seen to serve as a basis for reflection on each decision-making step in the context of the planning of a teaching–learning situation – although the starting point and end point are always the learners. As a result, a reflection question, for example, is not "Is what I plan challenging?" but "Is what I plan challenging for these learners?" At first glance, this may be a minor matter. At second glance, however, it becomes clear that it is essentially a different point of view and thus becomes a fundamental element of teacher professionalism. In order to think further about the example mentioned, the evaluation of the teaching–learning situation is not about whether teachers set the challenge but whether it has become visible to learners.

How can the models presented be brought together and used for further argumentation? The didactic hexagon is suitable for this. It can be found in all didactic models (more or less), it has an integrative character, and designates a structured organization of the essential elements of the planning of a teaching–learning situation (cf. Zierer, 2010).

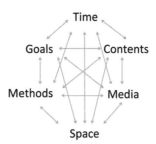

Figure 3.2

Following Werner Jank and Hilbert Meyer (2002), the question "Who should learn what, from whom, when and how long, with whom, where, how, with what, why and what for?" provides an overview of the content of this chapter:

- **Goals:** The questions about *who, why* and *what for* depend directly on each other, as the goals that a lesson sets always have to be seen in relation to students. This is called the first, important perspective.

- **Content:** Since goals always show up in specific situations and are therefore linked to content, the question *what* opens up another perspective.
- **Methods:** Due to the encounter between the teacher and the student in the material, lessons are always a mediation and in this respect a teaching–learning process. This is followed by the questions *who*, *with whom* and *how*, which must be answered from a methodological point of view with the help of forms of working and action, social forms, class and conversation management strategies, as well as teaching principles.
- **Media:** As it is often not possible to directly and immediately make the material to be conveyed experientially to the students, the question of what to use becomes significant. In this sense, media take on a mediator role between students and material and, furthermore, help enable learning through didactic preparation.
- **Space:** Classes usually take place in the classroom, and can also take place in corridors, gyms, auditoriums, on school playgrounds, online, or in almost all other rooms.
- **Time:** Even though everyday school life dominates a 45-minute lesson rhythm, for various reasons, the questions of *when* and *how long* concerning the lesson are not completely answered. For even these 45 minutes must be planned and coordinated with regard to the teacher, the student body, and the subject. Above all, considerations regarding the time structure of lessons offer numerous aids in order to be able to convey the time perspective adequately.

Goals, contents, methods, media, space, and time represent the central dimensions of teaching, which are also related to each other. This is what the double arrows in the previous figure try to indicate. The parallels with the "intentional alignment" approach are obvious (cf. Hattie, 2023). This will be pointed out and discussed again in the following sections.

3.1 GOAL PLANNING

Perhaps you have heard this statement: "Why should I worry about the goals of a lesson? You can find them in the curriculum!" Please take this position and reflect on the following questions: Do the goals in the curriculum always suit your class, your lessons and you? What is the relationship between the lesson's goals, the school's mission, and the subject? And how can goals be made visible to learners? In this section we want to deal with these questions and consider how the planning of the goals can be carried out in everyday school life and which evidence-based criteria can be used for this.

The following is one of the most interesting results of educational research: although teachers repeatedly emphasize how important goals are for learning success, they are not at the center of the considerations in lesson planning. Instead, method (e.g., choice of activities) and choice of media (e.g., laptops and tablets) decisions dominate. What are the reasons for this? An examination of common positions will get us started:

First, it is argued that the goals are given in the curricula and have therefore already been sufficiently reflected by curriculum makers. Without doubt, this is correct. Nevertheless: the learning effectiveness of goals is not generated at the curricular level; it is the responsibility of the teacher.

Second, there is a reason for the described situation in teacher education itself, as it takes place in many locations. In theory, it is emphasized in all phases that the formulation of goals is important, and in practical exams as well, prospective teachers are required to provide corresponding information in their lesson plans. In everyday school life, however, it becomes clear that the way in which goals are addressed can be optimized.

Third, it is not uncommon to hear teachers argue that goals have already been discussed in detail in previous lesson plans and do not need to be addressed again. However, it is overlooked that these goals have not yet been taught to specific learners in future lessons. In this respect, it cannot be assumed that the goals fit the performance level of the learners. Essentially, this reasoning reveals that experience does not always contribute to professionalization and can sometimes hinder it.

The consequence of these considerations can therefore be seen in communicating to teachers not just the competencies with regard to what successful goal formulation looks like. Rather, it is crucial to give them the attitude that evidence-based goal formulation is the basis for learning success.

Let us look again at the factors discussed in the previous section, which are directly related to the goals. There is much evidence that planning the goals essentially results in the task of a learning goal hierarchy, the operationalization of learning goals, and a learning goal taxonomy. These aspects are explained below and illustrated with some examples.

Although the "Learning hierarchies approach," with an effect size of 0.19, remains below the hinge point of 0.40, it is worth looking at, as it reveals when the formulation of goals becomes effective for education.

Classically, there are three levels in the hierarchy of learning goals. They should lead to clarity on the part of the teacher and help with the structuring of the goal formulation.

Figure 3.3

At the first level of the hierarchy are the general goals, based on how school and learning are defined. These include, for example, the general definition of the concept of education and also the articles on the pedagogical mandate of schools in individual country's constitutions as well as the preambles of the curricula. At the second level are the leading goals, which set the frame for the concrete goals of several lessons. In accordance with the hierarchical structure, leading goals depend on the general goals and must refer to them. Leading goals are so specific in their determination that they can be subjected to an immediate, i.e., direct, review. You can find them, for example, in subject curricula, such as mathematics, sciences, and foreign languages. And at the third level of the hierarchy are the specific goals that specify the goals for a single lesson.

With these considerations, two implications become apparent. First, when moving from general goals and learning goals to specific goals, the complexity decreases while the contextual relevance increases. Second, the number of goals may change accordingly: at the level of general goals, there may be fewer goals, which are then addressed by some specific goals. In practice, there is often talk of a rule of thumb, according to which a general goal is formulated for a lesson and specified with three to a maximum of six specific goals. The reason for this is that it makes little sense to set too many general goals or learning goals in one lesson and not achieve them. And whoever has achieved six specific goals in 45 minutes can be extremely satisfied. This rule of thumb can also be underpinned from a psychological perspective: according to George A. Miller (1956), only seven pieces of information, plus or minus two, can be retained in the short-term memory at the same time – but like most "rules of thumb" there can be many exceptions.

The secret of a successful hierarchy of learning goals lies in the linking of general goals, leading goals, and specific goals. This leads to clarity on the part of the teacher and learners. The teacher's clarity, as important as it is, must become learners' clarity: if the students do not understand the learning goals then these are likely to have less impact. Thus, the more specific the level of a learning objective hierarchy level and the greater the clarity and understanding on the part of learners, the greater the impact it will have on learning success.

The above remarks indicate that the formulation of goals is not a matter of course (cf. "Clear goal intentions," $d = 0.44$) – although everyone sets and achieves several goals in the course of their life without actually writing them down. However, many research projects have shown that there is definitely a qualitative difference in the formulation of learning goals, which is particularly evident when it comes to assessment of lessons: goals can only be checked if they are formulated in such a way that they can be checked. This addresses the learning objective of operationalization.

In this context, the study by Robert Mager (1962) is considered to be a classic, providing three postulates with regard to the formulation of learning goals:

1. Observable behavior on the part of the learner, which they should have mastered by the end of the lesson (e.g., writing down, calculating, reading), must be described.

2. Conditions under which the learner's behavior will be demonstrated (e.g., time limits, permitted or prohibited materials and equipment, permitted cooperation with other students) must be specified.
3. Criteria for success, according to which it can be decided whether and to what extent learners have achieved the objective, must be specified.

These three postulates (observable behavior, condition, criteria) were further differentiated by Gagné et al. (1992). An effective formulation of learning goals should therefore state:

1. Situation – describes the situation or context in which the learner's performance is to take place
2. Learned capability verb – is used to classify a learner's performance outcome.
3. Object – indicates the content of the learner's performance.
4. Action verb—indicates observable behavior through a description of how the learner's performance is to be completed.
5. Tools, constraints, or special conditions – specific equipment, temporal considerations, or the maximum number of attempts that a learner is allowed.

Finally, in objective setting theory, following Edwin Locke and Gary Latham (1990), goals should be SMART:

- **S**pecific, i.e., as precise as possible;
- **M**easurable, i.e., so that they can be checked;
- **A**ttractive, i.e., that are worth striving for and relevant;
- **R**ealistic, i.e., achievable; and
- **T**ime-phased, i.e., based on a specific period.

At this point you will notice that there are different variants of models. Yet the similarities prevail. In this respect, it is always better to orient oneself to one of these models than to none. Each of them has much supportive evidence.

The following table provides some examples of general and evidence-based operationalization of learning objectives. They are not perfect but are intended to illustrate what has been said.

General formulation	Evidence-based formulation
Students should know that water refracts light.	At the end of the lesson, students should be able to formulate a definition of the term "refraction" using the words "water," "light," "decompose," and "colors".
Students should know that light consists of different colors.	At the end of the lesson, students should be able to write down without further assistance that light consists of the five colors red, orange, yellow, green, and blue.
Students should know that when light falls on water a rainbow can be created.	At the end of the lesson, students should be able to fill in the blanks "If ... falls on ... then ... be able to be created."

This procedure may seem tedious at first glance and certainly costs teachers time, especially in their career-entry phase. However, it is the basis for any evaluation of lessons and is therefore essential: the more clearly the goals are formulated and the more they are understood by the students, then the greater the probability of learning success.

A number of suggestions are found in the literature. Among the best known are Bloom's taxonomy (1956), the Taxonomy of the German Education Council (1970), the SOLO taxonomy by Biggs and Collis (1982), and "Depth of Knowledge" (DOK) by Webb (1997).

Bloom (1956) based his taxonomy on the distinction that a learning objective has to be fleshed out with regard to two perspectives: its orientation and level. Orientation means the area of personality on which the learning objective focuses and accordingly relates to the following aspects:

- Cognitive aspects describe the knowledge of facts, concepts, principles, and procedures.
- Affective aspects relate to interests, needs, attitudes, evaluations, and approaches.
- Psychomotor aspects include the mastery of movement sequences and complex behaviors.

In contrast, the level differentiates the *complexity* of the learning goals, with the following levels of difficulty:

- **Knowledge** – if facts and information can be remembered.
- **Comprehension** – if facts and information can be processed and integrated into a larger context.
- **Application** – if facts and information can be used in a specific situation.
- **Analysis** – if a situation can be broken down into its components.
- **Synthesis** – provided that individual information can be combined into a larger whole.
- **Evaluation** – if judgments about facts and information can be made.

This overview clearly shows that Bloom's taxonomy can be associated with different competencies. In the following overview, an attempt is made to assign verbs to these levels of difficulty in order to be able to help with the formulation of learning goals. It should be noted that the use of a verb alone does not determine the level of difficulty:

Knowledge:

Enumerating, naming, describing, designating, defining, remembering, recognizing, determining, finding out, identifying, presenting, collecting, reproducing, repeating, quoting

Comprehension:

Expressing, distinguishing, selecting, expanding, reporting, decoding, differentiating, discussing, recognizing, explaining, contrasting, generalizing, pointing out, interpreting, clarifying, constructing, classifying, localizing, solving, estimating, translating, converting, predicting

Application:

Trying out, selecting, operating, calculating, assessing, obtaining, demonstrating, discovering, developing, adopting, using, interpreting, constructing, solving, planning, organizing, producing, testing, transferring, predicting, choosing

Analysis:

Deriving, arranging, executing, calculating, determining, relating, debating, differentiating, determining, experimenting, deducing, highlighting, identifying, illustrating, categorizing, classifying, criticizing, examining, investigating, comparing

Synthesis:

Accumulating, arraying, arranging, building, thinking, relating, setting up, developing, inventing, explaining, generalizing, generating, producing, integrating, categorizing, combining, constructing, creating, modifying, organizing, planning, collecting, transferring, preparing, suggesting, summarizing, merging, transferring

Evaluation:

Marking, assessing, evaluating, relating, recommending, deciding, interpreting, contrasting, criticizing, expressing an opinion, measuring, giving reasons, concluding, commenting, revising, convincing, differentiating, supporting, validating, comparing, insuring, defending

In 2001, a revision of Bloom's taxonomy titled "A Taxonomy for Teaching, Learning, and Assessment" was published by a collective of cognitive psychologists, curriculum theorists, instructional researchers, and testing and assessment specialists. The revision emphasizes dynamism by employing verbs and gerunds to label the six levels of knowledge, departing from the nouns used in the original taxonomy. These "action words" are used to articulate the cognitive processes through which individuals engage with and manipulate knowledge (cf. Anderson & Krathwohl, 2001, p. 76f.):

- Remembering: Retrieving, recognizing, and recalling relevant knowledge from long-term memory.
- Understanding: Constructing meaning from oral, written, and graphic messages through interpreting, exemplifying, classifying, summarizing, inferring, comparing, and explaining.

- Applying: Carrying out or using a procedure for executing or implementing.
- Analyzing: Breaking material into constituent parts; determining how the parts relate to one another and to an overall structure or purpose through differentiating, organizing, and attributing.
- Evaluating: Making judgments based on criteria and standards through checking and critiquing.
- Creating: Putting elements together to form a coherent or functional whole; reorganizing elements into a new pattern or structure through generating, planning, or producing.

Bloom's taxonomy has been recognized worldwide. It aligns with the considerations of the German Education Council (1970), whose taxonomy only distinguishes four levels:

- Reproduction: Reproduction of a single fact (sentences, definitions, formulas, rules, etc.).
- Reorganization: Application of several known facts or methods in a context familiar through practice.
- Transfer: Use of known facts or methods in a context which, while not fundamentally new, is varied and not yet familiar through corresponding practice.
- Problem-solving: Application of known facts or methods in a context unknown to learners; discovering or proving new facts.

This shows that the taxonomy of the German Education Council can be seen as a simplification of Bloom's taxonomy.

The SOLO model ("Structure of Observed Learning Outcomes"), which was developed by Biggs and Collis (1982), is also based on Bloom's taxonomy but nonetheless follows a different logic. It can be seen as a model of complexity and has five levels ranging from "not knowing" to expertise:

- Prestructural: No knowledge.
- Unistructural: Knowledge of one relevant aspect.
- Multistructural: Knowledge of several unrelated aspects.
- Relational: Knowledge of several related aspects.
- Extended abstract: Knowledge transferred to new facts.

While the first three levels relate to content or declarative knowledge and understanding, the last two levels relate to deeper or procedural understanding. Unlike the Bloom taxonomy, the SOLO taxonomy thus focuses on increasing complexity, including knowledge.

And finally, Norman L. Webb (1997) distinguishes four DOK levels:

Level 1 "Recall & Reproduction": Learners remember facts or reflect on an issue.

Level 2 "Skills & Concepts": Learners use appropriate knowledge and learned concepts in order to answer simple questions.

Level 3 "Strategic Thinking & Reasoning": Learners use appropriate knowledge and learned concepts in order to answer complex questions and explain phenomena.

Level 4 "Extended Thinking": Learners use their knowledge and skills to open up completely new tasks and topics.

A comparison of the models highlights their specific similarities:

	Bloom	**German Education Council**	**SOLO**	**DOK**
Surface level of understanding	Skills & Understanding	Reproduction	Unistructural	Recall & Reproduction
	Applying	Reorganization	Multistructural	Skills & Concepts
Deep level of understanding	Analysis & Synthesis	Transfer	Relational	Strategic Thinking & Reasoning
	Evaluation	Problem-solving	Extended Abstract	Extended Thinking

In the specialist literature there are various studies on the taxonomies mentioned, which also address advantages and disadvantages. There is a consensus that it is always better when planning lessons to have one taxonomy in mind than none at all (see Hattie, 2008, 2019). In order not to provoke excessive demands for everyday lesson planning, we recommend implementing at least the two levels "Surface level of understanding" and "Deep level of understanding." These can be quickly distinguished in terms of content and at the same time lay the foundation for the effectiveness of the target formulation. The argument is that there is much overlap *if* and only *if* the cognitive complexity of thinking and learning is considered.

We would like to clarify this with the "Goldilocks Principle," named after the famous children's story:

> A girl named Goldilocks comes into a house in which three bears live. Each of the three bears has his preferences in terms of eating, living, and sleeping. After the girl tests the food, a chair, and the bed of all three bears, she concludes that one bear's food is too hot, his chair is too big, and his bed is too hard. The other bear's food is too cold, his chair is too small, and his bed is too soft. Only one bear's food and chair and bed fits everything: it is "just right."

The main idea of the children's story is that there is always a midway point between extremes which best suits certain conditions. This effect has been demonstrated in various fields of science, including in medicine and in communication science. For example, a medication may be overdosed or underdosed. Ultimately, in many contexts, it is the golden mean or the right measure that decides whether success is possible – an idea that can be found in the work of Aristotle.

Applying this principle to school and lessons reveals a central insight: it is not very helpful for learning success to overwhelm a learner who is on the reproduction level with tasks on the transfer level. Likewise, it doesn't make much sense to overwhelm a learner who is on the problem-solving level with tasks on the reorganization level. Rather, it is important to achieve a fit between the requirement level on the one hand and the performance level on the other. If the teacher manages to do this, the challenge is set and the prerequisites are in place for achieving the greatest possible learning success. Similarly, the work should not be too hard, not too easy, and certainly not boring (cf. "Appropriately challenging goals," $d = 0.60$).

An optimal learning path also precedes the achievement of a certain objective. This applies in spite of different learning requirements across students. Successful differentiation does not mean that every learner has to be offered varying goals at all times and consequently different pathways: on the one hand, no teacher can do this every day, and on the other hand, research results show that this is not as effective as when learners work together on the same goals with learning opportunities tailored to their performance. The term learning path comes to mind here. There can be similar success criteria but differentiation means there can be differing times and progressions to get there – *not* different activities for different kids, which so often reify the expectations.

The prerequisite for this is that teachers appropriately diagnose the initial situation, are in constant exchange with learners, regularly evaluate lessons, and critically and constructively question their own approach. For the decision field of the goals, the following learning path can be created schematically:

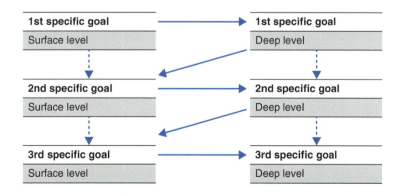

The following table provides another example for illustration and discussion:

	Surface understanding	**Deep understanding**
Leading goal	Students should study the diffusion of light in order to find out its composition and its alteration when it enters water.	Students can explain how the diffusion of light can be investigated and why light appears in different colors when it enters water.
1st specific goal	At the end of the lesson, the students should be able to formulate a sentence definition of the term "refraction" using the words "water," "light," "refraction," and "colors."	At the end of the lesson, the students should be able to formulate a sentence definition of the term "refraction" without further assistance.
2nd specific goal	At the end of the lesson, students should be able to write down without further assistance that light consists of the five colors red, orange, yellow, green, and blue.	Students should be able to explain at the end of the lesson why light shines red through a red film.
3rd specific goal	At the end of the lesson, students should be able to fill in the blanks "If ... falls on ... then ... will be able to be created."	At the end of the lesson, students should be able to explain in one sentence how a rainbow is created.

Successful teaching is characterized by the clarity of the teacher and the clarity of the learners, which together form the clarity of the lessons. Goals are crucial for this. In order to be able to differentiate the different perspectives at the level of action, we speak of goals on the one hand and success criteria on the other. In this respect, making one criterion visible is particularly worthwhile if the other criterion is also made visible.

A common question is when in the learning process is it necessary to inform the learner about the success criteria of the lesson? On the one hand, there are arguments that learning requires an arc of tension in order to motivate and become sustainable, and that it is better to let learners learn some of the lesson vocabulary so they better understand the success criteria. On the other hand, there are views that advocate making the learning objective and success criteria clear to learners as early as possible in the learning process (cf. "Goal commitment," $d = 0.44$).

The results of empirical teaching research indicate that at a certain point in the class it is necessary to make the success criteria visible and explicit to learners (cf. "Success criteria," $d = 0.64$). Not only do teachers need to know what the objective of the lesson is and when it has been achieved, but this knowledge needs to be shared with learners and made explicit, clear, and understood.

To clarify the connection but also the difference between goals and success criteria, in the following table we draw on one of the examples mentioned above.

Lesson content	3rd specific goal (deep level)	Necessary success criteria	Example
How is a rainbow created?	At the end of the lesson, students are expected to be able to explain in one sentence how a rainbow is created.	1. I know that light is made up of different colors. 2. I know that water refracts light. 3. I know that light can be broken down into its colors by refraction. 4. I know that when light falls on water, a rainbow can be created.	A rainbow is created when it rains and at the same time the sun shines on the rain at a 42-degree angle from the perspective of the beholder.

If this combination of goals and success criteria is now created not only for a lesson but for a lesson sequence, the following matrix is obtained, which has many similarities to so-called learning pathways and competence grids (cf. Hattie, 2019 p. 63).

Learning intentions success criteria

SOLO 1: Recognize that light and sound are types of energy that are detected by ears and eyes		
Uni-/multi-structural	Recognize that light/sound are forms of energy and have properties	I can name one/or more properties of light and sound
Relational	Know that sound/light can be transformed into other forms of energy	I can explain how light/sound is transformed into other types of energy
Extended abstract	Understand how light/sound allows us to communicate	I can discuss how light/sound enables us to communicate
SOLO 2: Be able to draw a normal, measure angles, and define the law of reflection		
Uni-/multi-structural	Be able to draw ray diagrams, including the normal, with correctly drawn angles	I can draw a ray diagram with correctly measured angles
Relational	Be able to define the Law of Reflection, linking the terms "incidence" and "reflected ray"	I can define the Law of Reflection, linking the terms "incidence" and "reflected ray," as well as "normal" and "smooth surface"
Extended abstract	Recognize that the Law of Reflection is true for all plane surfaces and can predict what will happen if the surface is rough	I can predict what will happen if light is reflected off a rough surface and explain why it happens

(Continued)

SOLO 3: Be able to use ray boxes to understand how concave and convex mirrors behave		
Uni-/multi-structural	Know that changing the distance of an object from a concave mirror changes the appearance of the image	I can recognize that an image in a concave mirror changes as an object is moved closer or farther away from the mirror
Relational	Be able to explain why concave mirrors are known as "converging mirrors" and convex mirrors as "diverging mirrors"	I can explain (using diagrams) why concave and convex mirrors are referred to as "convergent" and "divergent" mirrors, respectively
Extended abstract	Recognize patterns in reflected rays from concave and convex mirrors, and be able to make a generalization	I can write a generalization about the patterns of reflected rays in concave and convex mirrors

This example shows that goals and success criteria are decisive for learning success and have five teaching implications:

1. Challenge: The teaching of learning goals and success criteria leads to learners being able to better understand where they are in the learning process, where their strengths and weaknesses are, and where the dissonance between ability and not-yet-being-able can be seen. If this is misunderstood, it can lead to lack of engagement on the part of learners.
2. Voluntary commitment: When students share commitment to the success criteria, this can improve the rate of learning.
3. Self-confidence: Students' trust in their own performance is important for learning success. This is fed on the one hand by self-efficacy, social contacts, and having an understanding of where they are relative to the success criteria. Above all, teachers have the opportunity to show students what they can already do and where they have already made progress by visualizing goals and addressing the success criteria.
4. Expectations of the learners: As students learn to assess themselves they learn not to develop too high or too low expectations of themselves. When the goals have high commitment and the tasks are not seen as boring, this can allow students to realize even higher expectations of themselves – as our role is to help students exceed what they think are their expectations.
5. Conceptual understanding: Learning proceeds typically from a surface understanding to a deeper understanding. Neither one is more important or even better than the other. Rather, the one builds on the other and thus shows their interaction relationship. Understanding this interaction is what is called conceptual understanding. Learners who know what level they are at, why

this level is important, and what their next steps are can learn more effectively and sustainably. This is why Hattie and Clarke (2018) recommend that many lessons may need two success criteria – one for the content, facts, ideas, and knowledge, and one for the deeper relational and transfer thinking. Similarly there may be need for two activities, two assessment tasks, and multiple methods of teaching to ensure instructional alignment.

Finally, we would like to discuss the problem of whether it would be better to speak of teaching objectives instead of learning goals because the teacher formulates the goals and not the students (cf. Meyer, 2004). There are two reasons against this: on the one hand, it has now become established to speak of learning goals, since students are supposed to open up to them and thus have an understanding. It helps to "co-construct" the success criteria with the students, as then they can have a deeper understanding, but in reality the teacher creates the criteria as novices often do not know what they do not know nor what success looks like (given the time, opportunity, and resources).

This is achieved by a thorough analysis of the initial situation (based on excellent diagnosis of what students bring to the lesson in terms of their skills, wills, and motivations) and by transparency and clarity of goals. It is best done at the start of the lesson – for example, by writing the objective of the lesson on the board or – even better – formulated with students at the start of the lesson.

When conducting the lesson, i.e., in the phase of implementation, it is particularly important to ensure that the clarity of the goals on the part of the teacher also becomes clarity of the goals on the part of the learner. In this respect, at least, the learning goals and corresponding success criteria must be disclosed and made visible to learners.

Exercises

Surface level

1. Outline different models of learning hierarchy, learning objective operationalization, and learning objective taxonomy.

Deep level

2. Discuss the different models of learning goal hierarchy, operationalization of learning goals, and learning goal taxonomy. Identify differences and similarities and finally take a critical, constructive position on each model.
3. Plan the goals of one of your next lessons with colleagues and consider the learning goal hierarchy, operationalization of learning goals, and learning goal taxonomy. Please use the following placemat as a stimulus for the exchange. Each group member first thinks about how they would plan the lesson goals

and enters a suggestion on the sheet. The group members then read the suggestions on their own before the group comes together for an exchange of ideas. At the end of the exercise, an agreement is noted in the middle of the sheet and used for further planning. Transfer the results obtained in each case into the matrix that follows.

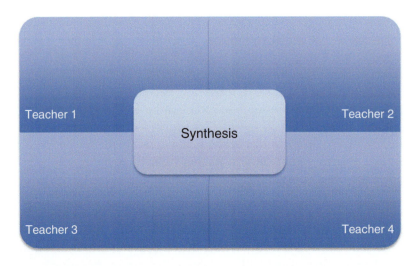

Learning goals matrix	
General Goals	
Leading Goals	
Surface Level	Deep Level
Specific Goals	
Surface Level	Deep Level
Success Criteria	
	Example

3.2 CONTENT PLANNING

It is one of the central questions of learners: "Why am I expected to learn this? Is it in the test?" Often they only hear the answer: "Because it is in the curriculum." But they want and need to know more. There is such an abundance of material in curricula that a central task of lesson planning is to make decisions about the knowledge and knowing for the lessons, and how to make it relevant to the lives of students. In this section, we want to deal with this issue and consider, based on evidence, what is worth noting about the planning of content and how this can be implemented in everyday school life.

When planning the content, it is important to pick up on and merge the three steps of the analysis of lesson content described in Chapter 2.

1. Subject matter analysis: From a subject matter point of view it is important to describe the lesson content using clear, challenging, and worthwhile goals for the lessons: "Clear goal intentions" ($d = 0.44$), "Goal commitment" ($d = 0.44$), and "Appropriately challenging goals" ($d = 0.60$).
2. Educational analysis: In this context, it is important to clarify why the content is being learned and for what purpose. The *why* speaks directly to engaging students' motivations: "Achieving motivation and approach" ($d = 0.44$) and "Deep motivation and approach" ($d = 0.58$) therefore play a role.
3. Learning analysis: Here, it is necessary to relate the new material to what students know already: "Prior ability & intelligence" ($d = 0.96$), "Prior achievement" ($d = 0.73$), and "Piagetian levels" ($d = 1.28$).

As convincing as each of these perspectives may be, the real challenge begins with the synthesis: How can the subject matter, educational, and learning analysis be brought together? What are the procedures that are effective?

The research results on the factor "Cognitive task analysis" ($d = 1.09$) are particularly significant. As with many procedures, there are a number of suggestions for implementation in the context of a cognitive task analysis. The following core idea is common: the breakdown of a task into a step-by-step procedure, first to meaningfully reduce the complexity of the task and second to adapt the task to the learning requirements of students. This is usually done in five steps:

1. Previous knowledge: Identification of key points of explaining and understanding.
2. Identification of knowledge representations: Generation and sequence of subtasks.
3. Application of methods for targeted knowledge gathering: Development of subtasks.
4. Analysis and review of the recorded data: Test run the subtasks and revise them if necessary.
5. Use of the results for learning processes: Implementation of the subtasks.

The research results on the factor "Scaffolding and situated learning" ($d = 0.52$) are equally important. Here, too, there are different models but the common denominator is the following:

1. Provision of a task sequence: Based on possible problems in explaining and understanding the lesson content, a task sequence is developed to be able to open up the facts.
2. Transparency of the meaningfulness of the lesson content: Learners are shown why it is important to understand the facts of the matter and why the associated tasks have to be worked on.

3. Control of the learning process: Although the learning process is carried out by learners, instructions are included in every step of the learning process to prevent a deviation from the learning objective.
4. Clarification of expectations: With the help of case studies, learners are shown when a task has been solved and which criteria are important in the subsequent assessment.
5. Providing help: To support the self-monitoring of the learning processes, materials are offered, which the learner can use if they get stuck.
6. Avoiding uncertainties, surprises, and disappointments: The sequence of tasks and the associated classroom discussion are tested step by step before the application to rule out possible problems in advance and ensure maximum learning success.

If the factors "Cognitive task analysis" ($d = 1.20$) and "Scaffolding" ($d = 0.52$) are compared, on the one hand there are many overlaps and cross-references to other factors. They guarantee the success of these factors. On the other hand, it also becomes clear that these procedures are time-consuming and therefore cannot be implemented by every teacher in every lesson. As a result, it will have to be clarified where the overlaps can be seen and why they are important in order to be able to use them to design a matrix for planning the content that can be used in everyday lesson planning and thus as efficiently as possible:

First, a logical sequence of the tasks makes sense. This prevents breaks in thinking and is necessary for correcting misconceptions, enabling a correct understanding of the matter. As a result, tasks have to be created which build on one another and enable a framework which – as Johann Amos Comenius (1657) indicated in his *Didactica Magna* – progresses from easy to difficult, from the known to the unknown, from the near to the distant. An appropriate linguistic framework that is planned and developed and evaluated by teachers prior to the implementation is an important strategy for this.

Second, the learning situation of students must be brought into line with the level of the tasks. Like the goals, these can address surface understanding or deep understanding, ranging from reproduction to problem-solving. According to the "Goldilocks Principle," the challenge level of the tasks should be not too easy, not too difficult, and not too boring – or, as informed by cognitive load theory, a high intrinsic (subject-related) load combined with a low extrinsic (non-subject) load is most effective for learning.

Third, the form of the representation is significant. Jerome Bruner (1966) essentially differentiated three forms: enactive (action based), iconic (image based), and symbolic (language based).

- Enactive: Knowledge is acquired *action based* with specific material that represents the subject of the lesson.
- Iconic: Knowledge is acquired *image based*, by dealing with material that represents the specific action in an image.
- Symbolic: Knowledge is acquired by dealing with material that converts the specific action into *symbols*.

As research results show, it is advantageous for learning if students have to work out the subject of a lesson using different forms of representation and, depending on their level of proficiency, it is better for them if one of the forms of representation mentioned above is at the center of the learning process. This has consequences for the question of media, since the forms of representation not only describe how to deal with the subject matter but also provide information about the learning materials, as the examples given above for the mathematics lesson also show. Each of these forms of representation is therefore important for learning and therefore should be taken into account when planning the content.

Fourth, the burden on working memory when creating tasks has to be considered. If, for example, learning materials are peppered with unnecessary information, characterized by confusion, and littered with a flood of cross-references, the working memory load increases in this area.

Fifth, questions of motivation must be addressed. Often teachers tend not to reflect on the *why* question from the students' perspective. In the classroom and throughout the lesson, however, it is important to flesh out the reasons for the goals and the content, combining this with the learning requirements of learners. Motivation has four dimensions, which teachers can influence through appropriate motivational strategies (cf. Keller, 2010):

- Attention can be generated, for example, by creating a conflict between prior knowledge and an observation.
- Relevance can be created, for example, by providing the topic of the lesson with present or future significance.
- Confidence can be generated, for example, by presenting tasks that the learner can (just about) achieve or by building self-confidence.
- Satisfaction can be generated, for example, by encouraging positive developments or unexpectedly giving recognition.

In the following table, a number of motivational strategies are assigned to the dimensions mentioned.

\multicolumn{4}{c}{**Motivation strategies**}
Attention	**Relevance**	**Confidence**	**Satisfaction**
Incompatibility/ Making conflict	Satisfy needs	Properties/attributes	Making natural consequences tangible
Being specific	Current value	Self-confidence	Avoiding negative influences
Guarantee variability	Future benefit	Structuring according to difficulty	Strengthening positive developments
Humor	Experience	Expectations	Articulating expectations and making them realizable
Asking again	Options	Learning requirements	Allowing unexpected distinctions

How can these considerations be summarized so that they can be taken into account in everyday lesson planning? We recommend the following task analysis matrix, which we believe brings to light the results of the empirical pedagogical research and converts them into a working model.

Dimension	Characteristic		
Sequence of content	Beginning	Middle	End
Cognitive level	Simple (Reproduction and Reorganization)	Middle (Transfer)	Difficult (Problem-solving)
Form of representation	Enactive	Iconic	Symbolic
Complexity of the task	Low	Average	High
Connecting to real-life problems (motivation)	High	Average	Low

At this point, we will discuss another factor that clarifies how important it is to bring together and summarize knowledge gained. This is the factor "Outlining and summarization," which has an effect size of 0.62. Although this factor mainly examines a number of strategies that emphasize the self-monitoring of the learning process, there is no doubt that it can be supported in class by the role model of the teacher. Learning from the role model is not only an effective way to acquire knowledge and skills in infancy, but it is also one of the most important and successful ways of learning across all lifetimes. Against this background, the challenge for the teacher is to specify the steps of the content as well as the goals and success criteria of the lesson.

In the last step of content planning, the task is to align the considerations and create a discussion guide. The objective of this discussion guide is to provide learners with systematic and reflective instructions, prompts, and supports for developing lesson content. By anticipating dialogues, the crucial points in the learning process can be discussed. Hence, a discussion guide is an attempt to see learning through the eyes of students. The instructions, prompts, and supports must always be designed so that they are not over- or under-complicated, but are always challenging so that learners can just about master the challenges by themselves. A discussion guide is one of the central elements for effectiveness both in the case of the factors "Scaffolding and situated learning" ($d = 0.52$) and "Cognitive task analysis" ($d = 1.09$) as well as the factors "Worked examples" ($d = 0.47$) and "Planning and prediction" ($d = 0.83$).

At the end of the planning of the content, one aspect that deserves special mention is the implemented plans. As a result, it is important to go through your own planning steps again.

Exercises

Surface level

1. Outline the essential steps in the planning of the lesson content.

Deep level

2. Plan the content of one of your next lessons with colleagues. Develop tasks based on the goals and analyze them using the task analysis matrix. Then develop a discussion guideline, entering it in the table below. Transfer your ideas into the planning concept map at the end of the section. Use the following placemat as a stimulus for the exchange. Each group member first thinks about how they would develop the tasks and enters a suggestion on the sheet. The group members then read the suggestions on their own before the group comes together for an exchange of ideas. At the end of the exercise, an agreement is noted in the middle of the sheet and used for further planning.

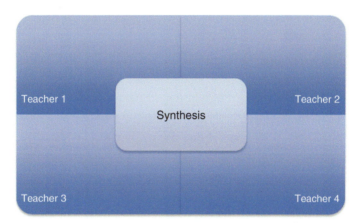

Task analysis matrix

Dimension	Task 1	Task 2	Task 3	Task 4
Sequence of content (start – middle – end)				
Cognitive level (easy – moderate – difficult)				
Representation form (enactive – iconic – symbolic)				
Complexity of the task set (low – average – high)				
Connecting to real-life problems (high – average – low)				

Discussion guideline

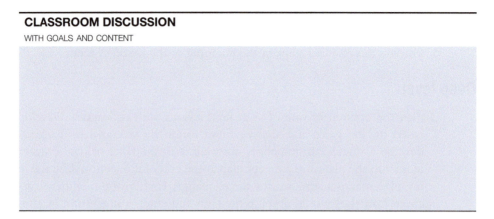

Planning concept map (blackboard illustration, PPT slides, etc.)

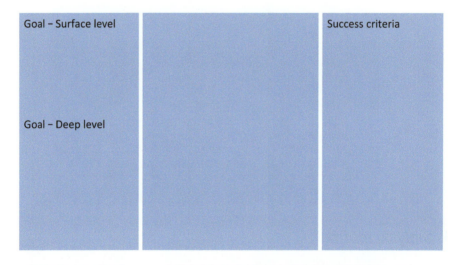

Figure 3.4 Planning Concept Map (blackboard illustration, PPT slides etc.)

3.3 METHOD PLANNING

Hardly any other topic is discussed as passionately as the question of method: Is it better to choose methods that show learners the way or to choose methods that take learners by the hand to where they are going? Every teacher has an opinion on this, based on their convictions, evaluations, and attitudes. Please answer the following questions for yourself: Which methods do you prefer? What reasons do you have for this preference: Are you led by personal preferences or expectations directed at you by the college or research results? What criteria do you use to select your methods? And how do you check the effectiveness of your choice? In this section, we want to discuss this issue and, based on evidence, consider what is worth noting about the planning of methods and what conclusions for preparing the lessons can be drawn from this.

A widespread belief is that a good lesson runs smoothly, with learners occupied for as long as possible, using as many different methods as possible. Such lessons certainly have the effect of being seen as organized and structured. But they are not necessarily good lessons. Now can it be concluded from such nice-looking lessons that all learning goals have been achieved? As an illustration of this, we would like to cite the following anecdote from teacher training.

Many pre-service teachers are asked to demonstrate lessons that include individual work, partner work, and group work. In addition to these activities, the lesson should also feature a lecture by the teacher, a student presentation, and a class discussion. If the pre-service teacher succeeds in incorporating all of these methodological elements into the classroom, then this demonstration lesson is given top marks, with the reason that the variety of methods used was visible!

In this example, however, the focus is directed to the wrong place: much more important than the variety of the methods is the success of the methods used, the impact on student learning, and thus the achievement of goals. So, the crucial questions in the demonstration lessons should be: First, did the methods used help to achieve the learning goals, and second was it possible to provide documentary proof of this impact? Evidence becomes the criterion of the question of method.

Haigh et al. (2013) asked 30 mentor teachers and initial teacher education lecturers to devise 20 questions they would ask in the following scenario to judge whether the teacher candidate is ready to teach: "I'd like you to imagine that a colleague has come to you seeking advice about whether their teacher candidate should pass practicum. She is trying to decide if the teacher candidate is ready to teach." The table on p. 81

Questions used to assess pre-service teachers' readiness to teach

	Learning as a teacher	**Personal qualities**	**Relationships**
Personal attributes	Are they able to act on feedback? Do they reflect critically on their own practice? Knowledge and planning	Do they have the necessary personal qualities/dispositions for teaching? Enacting teaching and management	How effective are their relationships with the children, staff, and parents? Assessment and use of evidence
Professional practices	Do they know the content/pedagogy of the teaching areas? Is their planning appropriately leveled and detailed?	Are they organized and prepared? Can they manage the classroom effectively?	Do they gather information about children's progress and use this in their teaching?

illustrates Haigh et al.'s coding of the 600 (30 × 20) questions. Do you see the core missing question?

Not once was the following core question asked: "Do the students learn?" The focus was on the *how* of teaching, on personal attributes, and on control and technique, and this overshadowed whether the teacher has had an impact on any or all students.

This perspective shows that no single right teaching method exists, and the focus needs to be on the impact of the methods. In German-speaking countries, in particular, a passionate discussion between supporters of open classrooms and advocates of traditional instruction can be observed, which becomes obsolete against the background of what has been said above: neither is open classroom per se better than traditional instruction, nor is open classroom per se worse than traditional instruction. It depends on whether or not the lesson has led to goal achievement. If teachers succeed in leading all students to learning success with monotonous teaching, then it was good teaching. But students deserve better than boring … hence the claims in this chapter.

It is the case that it is easier to provide evidence of whether or not a method has been used successfully than it is to collect evidence demonstrating that the chosen teaching method has had the desired impact on all students.

No single method will suffice, hence the plea for evidence-based diversity of methods. If the first teaching method used has had little impact, then it is necessary to change the method. Evidence based does not mean choosing the one method that performs best; rather, it involves considering how your implementation, the dispositions of your students, and the focus of your learning intentions may require alternative and diverse methods. In this context, evidence-based practice focuses on the data you collect from applying your method, hence the mantra "know thy impact." This evidence includes observations of individual and group work, the processing of worksheets or tasks, student comments, their views on the impact of the method, and conversations with parents. It is the triangulation of this evidence that allows you to make informed interpretations about the impact of your teaching method. Analyzing these effects, connecting them with your own reflections, and using empirical research results are essential elements of being evidence based in the sense of Visible Learning. In this regard, it's not about collecting more data but about effectively using the existing data to improve the quality of your teaching.

An important question is, "Why was the particular method used?" More often than not the responses include: "It has worked before for me," "I like this method," "The students were happy, manageable, and like this way of teaching," "This is the school's/inspector's/examination board's recommended method." But is it the best of the available methods?

The choice of method can primarily be judged in terms of its impact on the learning lives of the students; it is not the teaching that is decisive but the learning. It is the impact of the teaching that provides the justification for the choice of method. In this respect, there is a critical interaction between teaching quality and choice of method. Quality refers to the fidelity, dosage, and quality of the implementation, which is continually adjusted in light of the impact of the teaching method on the student's learning and their achievement of the success criteria.

The evergreens

As large as the number of methods and media has become and as numerous as the studies are, there is a combination of factors that can be claimed to be efficacious regardless of the age of learners, their performance level, the subject, and the type of school. In this sense, therefore, they are didactically methodical evergreens! Even if there are pitfalls that need to be considered with each of these factors (particularly in terms of implementation fidelity), the potential is enormous and it is recommended to use these methods as often as feasible.

Factor	d
Classroom discussion	0.82
Feedback	0.51
Peer tutoring	0.66
Questioning	0.49
Worked examples	0.47
Deliberate practice	0.49
Mnemonics	0.65
Practice testing	0.49
Rehearsal and memorization	0.71
Time on task	0.46
Cooperative learning	0.53
Direct instruction	0.56
Overall effect	0.57

The challengers

In addition to the "The Evergreens" combination of factors just mentioned, there are also a number of factors that have a lot of potential – but they need to be considered relative to age, nature of the tasks (content or deeper thinking), and probably in combination with other methods (such as those above).

Factor	d
Concept mapping	0.62
Self-verbalization/self-questioning	0.62
Discovery-based teaching	0.27
Homework	0.29
Inductive teaching	0.60
Jigsaw method	1.20
Problem-based learning	0.45
Overall effect	0.57

The dialogue promotors

Teaching is a person-to-person encounter. This philosophical reflection is supported by convincing empirical evidence. Several factors point to the need to regard teaching as an interaction between people, as a dialogue. Many of the following methods privilege interactions between teachers and students, or between students.

Factor	d
Collaborative learning	0.45
Decreasing disruptive behavior	0.82
Strong classroom cohesion	0.66
Peer- and self-grading	0.54
Scaffolding and situated learning	0.52
Small group learning	0.45
Overall effect	0.57

The confidence builders

The clarity and confidence students have in teachers are critical to the success of teaching methods, as is whether the feedback provided is heard, understood, and actionable. Students sense when teachers have high expectations for them all, whether they have deficit thinking or love labeling to explain why their teaching methods do not work, and whether teachers like them as people. Learning requires trust and confidence, as well as a positive culture toward making errors.

Factor	d
Teacher clarity	0.85
Teacher credibility	1.09
Teacher estimates of achievement	1.29
Teacher expectations	0.58
Teacher–student relationship	0.62
Teachers not labeling students	0.61
Overall effect	0.84

The self-regulated learners

By expanding the dataset to over 21,000 meta-analyses, a combination of factors appears critical: learners have to see themselves as their own teachers! This is what we mean by self-regulation. It is when students know what to do when they do not know what to do and encounter challenges. A variety of factors underpin this focus. In the 18th century, August Hermann Niemeyer, one of the founding fathers of education as a science in Germany, formulated a maxim for education and teaching: "I no longer need you!" Similarly, at the beginning of the 20th century, Maria Montessori summed up her main idea: "Help me to do it myself!" And in *Visible Learning for Teachers*, Hattie (2019) says: "The teacher must have the skills to get out of the way when learning approaches the criteria for success." And: "The goal of school is to make the learners their own teachers" (p. 14f.). Teachers need to learn to gradually release responsibility for teaching and learning, but in a deliberate, planned, and evaluative manner. Successful teachers enter the classroom with the attitude of a director who leads their class responsibly and humanely. Successful teachers do not face their class in an authoritarian way, according to which they decide everything by themselves and set the tone. Rather, they gently and appropriately introduce the students to the success criteria in a constant exchange of goals, content, methods, and media. They exchange ideas with their colleagues about ways, detours, and wrong turns, cooperate with parents, and approach the goal step by step with the students. However, ultimately each learner must master the learning content for themselves.

Factor	d
Effort management	0.77
Elaboration and organization	0.75
Evaluation and reflection	0.75
Help seeking	0.73
Self-control	0.66
Self-monitoring	0.50
Self-explanation	0.54
Overall effect	0.67

Despite all the interdependencies, Wolfgang Klafki's (1996) position remains that there is ultimately a primacy of goals. In other words, decisions about goals and content selection are not only more effective in terms of learning but also in terms of education. The intentional alignment approach supports this view: defining learning goals first and then aligning teaching methods with those goals is essential to maximizing educational outcomes (cf. Hattie, 2023). Given this context, the considerations from the previous chapter should be integrated with these decisions. In essence, alongside the formulation of goals at various levels, tasks were designed to maximize the success of achieving these goals. Both elements were incorporated into a discussion guideline, which now needs to be expanded to include the decision-making process regarding the choice of methods. Each of the models mentioned can serve as a justification for this approach.

In this book, we have selected the 7 C's based on their grip and empirical basis (cf. MET, 2010).

Reasons and method

Challenge:
Performance expectation, promotion of willingness to work hard, perseverance, and persistence

Control:
Efficient class management, active use of time, adherence to rules

Care:
Encouragement, emotional care, and support

Confer:
Promoting and granting of student assessments, acceptance of student feedback

Captivate:
Developing and maintaining fascination for the subject

Clarify:
Clarity, transparency, various explanations and approaches

Consolidate:
Consolidation, safeguarding, summary, feedback

For example, if a teacher opts for cooperative learning, we recommend not arguing:

"I choose cooperative learning because …"

Instead, it seems more meaningful to say:

"Dialogue in class is important to me to reach this success criteria, which is why …"

At first glance, it may seem trivial whether one starts to argue in this way or that. At second glance, however, taking the quality of teaching as a starting point ensures from the start that it is not the method that decides the goals or possibly becomes the myth of the debate, but the goals that point the way. The question of *why* is more important because it is more effective than the question of *what*. In this respect, what teachers do is not critical; it is much more important why they do something. So how teachers think about what they do is the key to success.

It is obvious that in the context of everyday lesson planning not all decisions that have to be made are reflected in every detail. This would overwhelm any teacher given the hours they have to plan on average each day. But the recommendation is to reflect on these decisions, at least for the most important steps in the classroom. If a teacher then determines that they can answer fewer than four of the 7 C's for a decision about the method, then it is worth questioning the choice of method made.

Differentiation means similar success criteria for all students but allowing for different ways and different times to get there. Some students may not reach the goal in the time available but that does not mean lowering the goal and moving to the next one – as then the gap can amplify. Differentiation does not mean different activities for different students, as so often this then means students are deliberately left behind, the attainment gap magnifies, and students are more aware of these lowering expectations. In this respect, learning pathways (note the plural as there is no one right pathway) must be addressed once again, which lead to suitable teaching and learning arrangements for varying goals and thus open up various learning pathways. These must be linked to the learning situation of the learner and adapted to the further learning process (cf. Hattie, 2019, p. 88). The prerequisite for this is that teachers appropriately diagnose the initial situation, are in constant exchange with learners about their learning progress, regularly evaluate the lessons, and critically and constructively question their own approach. This once again underlines the primacy of the teaching methods aligned with the students' starting and desired end points for the lesson rather than overly depending on one single teaching method. The following figure illustrates what has been said:

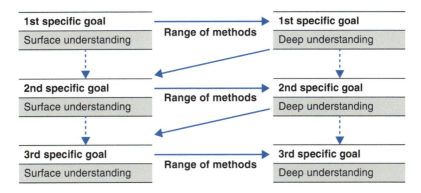

To conclude this section, we will address a factor that repeatedly is the subject of public debate: homework. With an effect size of 0.32 (but closer to zero in elementary school) it falls short of the much hoped for expectations of many that there is sufficient evidence to ban homework from school and teaching. We do not share this view but advocate for homework. So, what is the purpose of homework from an evidence-based perspective?

The complaint that children and adolescents often sit in front of their homework for hours and do not know how to do it, thinking it is more about completing anything than learning the best ways to be successful, is certainly justified – but it would be wrong to conclude that homework per se is bad. The power of homework is the opportunity to deliberately practice something already taught. This may mean you need to ensure students know about "deliberate practice" – that is, practice with feedback, not drill and kill. Any homework that requires assistance from another person (parent, sibling, tutor) loses its impact, and often confirms for the student that they are not smart at school and home.

Homework has little effect when learners spend so much time doing it exhaustively – the length of homework is not an important consideration, so keep it generally brief. When homework becomes "drilling and killing," i.e., mindless repetition without a challenge, it cannot be much more than a waste of time. The latter occurs especially when teachers do not explain homework and learners take forever to understand what is required of them. Furthermore, if the homework is not even addressed in the following lessons (integrated into the next lesson, marked, and feedback provided), then the effects can take a negative turn because demotivation can result, resulting in negative emotions. There is accumulating evidence that homework involving parents can have a negative effect (Hattie, 2023, p. 125f.), often because the parents either end up doing the homework or put pressure on the child to feel that they are not smart. Incidentally, these negative emotions can also arise when teachers introduce an extrinsic reward for completing homework – for example, when homework is given to learners as a kind of gift because the weather is nice or because currently there are holidays on the horizon. Homework is then stigmatized and has a negative connotation. But when homework is seen as a form of deliberate practice, serving both the preparation and the follow-up of the lesson; is challenging, regular, and diverse; and exposes important mistakes in the learning process that are then worked on in the next few lessons, then it can be a worthwhile adjunct to a successful lesson.

The reason the effects of homework are higher in high school than elementary school is that there is more deliberate practice of homework in high schools. However, it should be noted that many students need to be taught the learning strategies and skills of completing homework at school because if they do not have these skills, then they are unlikely to learn them themselves at home! In this respect, homework, meaningfully integrated into the lesson and focused on deliberate practice, is important in order to design learning processes successfully.

Exercises

Surface level

1. Outline the essential steps in the planning of methods.

Deep level

2. Supplement your guide to classroom discussion from the previous section with considerations on the choice of method and the reasons given. Plan these steps together and consider why you would use particular methods for each new step in the classroom discussion. Once again, use a placemat as a stimulus for

the exchange. Each group member first thinks about how they would choose a method and makes a suggestion on the sheet. The group members then read the suggestions on their own before the group comes together for an exchange of ideas At the end of the exercise, an agreement is recorded in the middle of the sheet and used for further planning. Transfer the results obtained in each case to the table below.

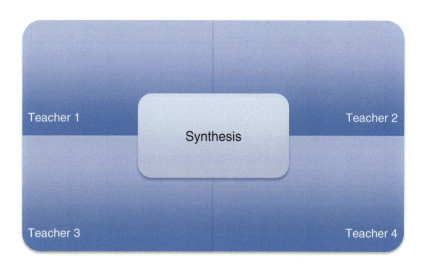

CLASS DISCUSSION
WITH GOALS AND CONTENT

Reasons Given
For Methods

Challenge
Control
Care
Confer
Captivate
Clarify
Consolidate

3.4 MEDIA PLANNING

The attention given to digitalization is intensive in society as well as in education. Opinions often diverge and at least two camps quickly form: while some are of the opinion that digital media can revolutionize learning, others believe that analogue media are better for pedagogical success. Where do you position yourself in this debate – on the side of the digitalization euphoric or the side of the digitalization apocalyptic? But more important than this positioning are your reasons. In this section, we want to discuss the research, considering what is worth noting about the planning of media and what conclusions can be drawn for class preparation.

Media have always been the subject of school and teaching (from slates to books, television, computers, etc.). In current debates, the importance of media is increasing because many believe that digitalization changes everything – including school and teaching. A lot of money is being invested in the acquisition of technology; it is not going away, but is more likely to become more pervasive in our lives (cf. Zierer, 2019).

In view of the fact that the current dataset of Visible Learning contains a number of factors that deal with the effectiveness of digital media, the following key questions will be considered (cf. Zierer, 2019): What influence on learning success does digital media have depending on (1) the age of the learners, (2) the subject, and (3) the technology?

Regarding point (1), the effect sizes of the factors on digitalization with elementary students ($d = 0.44$), high school students ($d = 0.30$), and college students ($d = 0.34$) show that there is neither a steady increase nor a steady decrease in effectiveness. This would be the prerequisite for drawing the conclusion that there is a correlation between age level and the influence of digitalization on learning success. An example in this context is the factor "Cooperative learning," which achieves higher effects with increasing age of the learners (cf. Hattie & Zierer, 2019; Zierer, 2019). Thus, the effectiveness of digital media does not depend on the age of the learners.

Concerning point (2), the factors concerning digital media in the context of subject learning yield the surprising result that digitalization achieves only low effect sizes in the natural sciences ($d = 0.18$) and mathematics ($d = 0.37$) – both subjects that can be described as having an affinity for digitalization. The values for reading ($d = 0.26$) and writing ($d = 0.41$) appear equally low – there are obvious pitfalls in the use of media in these areas, as encompassed in the factor "Use of smartphones and tablets in the classroom." In the case of reading, there is only a small effect. In comparison, the effect size of 0.55 in foreign language teaching is considerable. Thus, the effectiveness of digital media does not depend on the subject.

Regarding point (3), one of the most persistent arguments in the discussion about the possibilities and limits of digitalization in education is that it is only a matter of time before technology revolutionizes learning. But the data from

Visible Learning suggest that this is not automatic. This is because the more recent achievements of the digital age include "Online seminars" ($d = 0.14$), "One-on-one laptops" ($d = 0.16$), "Clickers" ($d = 0.21$), "Distance or online education" ($d = 0.25$), and "Webinars" ($d = 0.33$) – all with small effects on learning success. The factor with the highest effect size is "Interactive video/multimedia" ($d = 0.54$). Thus, the effectiveness of digital media does not depend on whether the medium is newly invented or already established.

Given the influence of learners' age, subject, and technology on the effectiveness of learning with digital media, what general results can be stated? Since no correlations can be derived from the data in all three aspects, it can be assumed that they are not decisive in the success of digitalization. Instead, the following conclusion points in a decisive direction: more important than the age level or the subject or the technology is the question of how the teacher succeeds in integrating digital media into the classroom. This puts the quality of teaching, and thus teacher professionalism, at the center of digitalization in the education system. Digital media do not turn bad lessons into good ones. Only good teaching can benefit from it.

Here is a chance to note the increasing impact of social media on learning. While the presence of mobile phones and social media such as as Facebook, Instagram or Snapchat can be distracting ($d = -0.25$), they could particularly help students to discuss what they do not know and to engage in error detection and correction. The effect size is 0.50.

Despite these findings, there is always an argument that what has been said applies only to the hardware and software from five or ten years plus ago, whereas the latest achievements of the computer age have already gone one step further and have now addressed all the previous objections. But here too the results of empirical pedagogical research tell a different story. For example, if you take all of the above-mentioned factors from Visible Learning, which are to be located in the context relative to the year of publication, the resulting picture is as follows (see Figure 3.5).

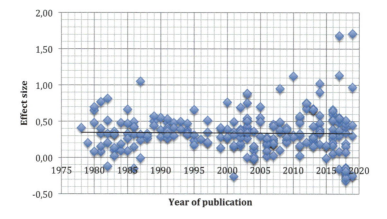

Figure 3.5 Effect of digital media over the years.

Figure 3.5 shows (apart from a large scatter) a constant average effect size over the past 40 years, despite the improvement in technology. The conclusion is that the impact of technology is more dependent on the quality of teaching and thus on the professionalism of the teacher. It is not the medium itself that guides the choice of media, but rather teachers' expertise in using technology as part of successful learning.

With this in mind, the recommendation is given to start with *why* and not *what*, i.e., to answer the media question based on the teaching quality.

Reasons and media

Challenge:
Performance expectation, promotion of willingness to make an effort, endurance, and persistence

Control:
Efficient classroom management, active use of time, observance of rules

Care:
Encouragement, emotional care and support

Confer:
Promotion and granting of student assessments, assumption of student feedback

Captivate:
Develop and maintain fascination for the subject

Clarify:
Clarity, transparency, varied declarations and additions

Consolidate:
Consolidation, safeguarding, summary, feedback

In this respect, it is not advisable to argue:

"I opt for a QR code because …"

Instead, it seems more appropriate to say:

"Dialogue in class is important to me, which is why I use a digital tool via a QR code for collaboration …"

Again, at first glance it may seem trivial whether one starts to argue in this way or another. At second glance, however, a different perspective emerges. If you take the quality of the lessons as a starting point, this ensures from the beginning that the media used do not dictate the goals, but instead that the goals show the way. The question of *why* is more important because it is more effective than the question of *what*. In this respect, what teachers do is not critical; it is much more important why they do something.

During the COVID-19 pandemic, one of the most important pedagogical policy tasks was not only to bring schools online but also to equip them with the associated latest technology. This process is ongoing as new technology emerges, such as ChatGPT, and challenges the school system again and again. There is no Ministry of Education that has not started an initiative in this area. All federal states have set out to turn schools into digital learning institutions, providing a lot of money for them to do so. For many, digital media are the decisive step driving education in the 21st century. The hope is that learning becomes easy. This is where the problem begins in this context, as numerous empirical pedagogical research studies have shown: simply upgrading schools with computers, tablets, and smartboards does not revolutionize learning. As shown above, digital media do not go beyond effect sizes between 0.2 and 0.4. None of the technical achievements change the grammar of the learning, which is particularly evident in the fact that learning is hard work. In addition, the reasons for these low effects are obvious: the provision of digital media alone does not cause teachers to change their teaching style and then exploit the potential of digital media. Rather, digital media are primarily used as a replacement for traditional media: the computer as a lexicon replacement, the tablet as a worksheet replacement, and the smartboard as a replacement for the blackboard.

However, it is certainly not only because of the teachers that the new media cannot (yet) produce the effects that many hope for. There is also a shortcoming in the programs themselves that come into the classrooms with the new media. Frequently optically and acoustically overloaded, with blinking here and popping there, they lead to a "cognitive overload," which in turn overloads the working memory. As already mentioned, euphoric proponents of digital media like to argue that the objections mentioned are quite justified – but this only applies to the older hardware and software, whereas the latest achievements of the computer age have already gone a step further and have addressed the concerns raised. But here too the research speaks a different language, showing that progress cannot resolve the objections mentioned. The latest technology also needs people who can operate it, and today's programmers are not immune to misdirecting the existing programming options. We have been waiting for a corresponding digital revolution in education for over 20 or 30 years, so one is inclined to conclude that it will not come in this form either.

"Pedagogy before technology!" is the motto. This challenges the frequently found message of new media. From a technical point of view, it may well be a matter of designing learning processes in such a way that they become "easier" – yes, this idea may even be useful for the teacher. But this message is wrong for learners because learning is only easy for the individual in rare cases, and definitely not in general. In this respect, the aim must rather be to make it clear to the students that commitment and effort are helpful for learning processes. It is only against this background that the importance of digital media becomes clear: they help learners to push themselves to the limit, can make mistakes visible in a different, special way, and under certain circumstances clearly show where there are mistakes in the learning process. An example is a sports teacher who records the movement sequence of a student on video and then enters an exchange with them, plays the film back and forth, goes through it in slow motion, and stimulates cognitive processes that would not be possible with traditional media. In this respect, digital media have the potential not only to act as an information carrier but also to be used for information processing.

This insight into the effectiveness of media can be used didactically in the so-called SAMR model, which was designed by Ruben R. Puentedura (2018). It can be combined with the empirical findings from Visible Learning and comprises the following four phases, from which the above-mentioned acronym is derived (cf. Zierer, 2019):

1. At the "Substitution" level, digitalization is used as a replacement for traditional media, without any corresponding added value being recognizable or even being demanded.

    Example: Learners write a story on the computer instead of writing it with paper and pencil. The learner continues to be on their own.
2. At the "Augmentation" level, digitalization is understood as an extension of traditional media by combining several forms of traditional media, and the digital connection means added value is possible in terms of speed and availability.

    Example: Learners use spelling and grammar checks, as well as a thesaurus on the computer, which would otherwise require several books. Again, the learner continues to be on their own.
3. At the "Modification" level, digitalization is used to change tasks in a way that would not be possible with traditional media.

    Example: Learners not only write a story but a script that they are then expected to implement in a team. This leads to social and cognitive networking because, first, several learners are working on a common cause, and second, further requirements (narrator perspective, camera setting, audio track, image sequence, handling of technology, etc.) have to be considered.
4. At the level of "Redefinition," there is also a new assignment of the task with regard to communicative and content networking.

    Example: Learners not only make the film for the screenplay in a team but also use digital media to share the film with people who cannot come together in the same place and at the same time. This can be an author or a director. This increases social and cognitive networking once again.

As this brief description of the levels of digitalization shows, the change from information carrier to information processing is recognizable. If one transfers this idea to an evidence base following Visible Learning, it can be argued that an effect size below 0.4 can be expected on the first and second levels, if new media are compared with traditional media. It gets more interesting at the third and fourth levels, where effect sizes above 0.4 can be achieved (cf. Zierer, 2019).

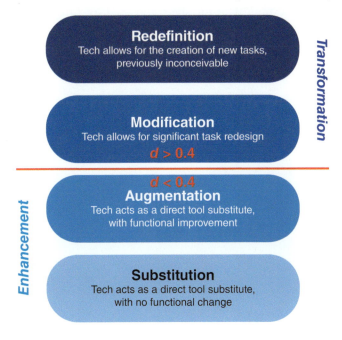

Figure 3.6 SAMR model and effect sizes.

In this respect, digitalization has key possibilities: the better teachers succeed in using new media in such a way that they change and reassign previous tasks with regard to the requirement level and communication, the greater will be the impact on students' learning performance. In short, teaching quality is crucial.

Exercises

Surface level

1. Outline essential steps in the planning of the use of media.

Deep level

2. In addition to your guideline for classroom discussion from earlier in this chapter, complete the following, considering the choice of media. Plan these steps with colleagues and consider why you would use a particular form of media for each new step in the class discussion. Again, use a placemat as a

stimulus for the exchange. Each group member first thinks about how they would plan the use of media and enters a suggestion on the sheet. The group members then read the suggestions on their own before the group comes together for an exchange of ideas. At the end of the exercise, an agreement is noted in the middle of the sheet and used for further planning. Transfer the results obtained in each case into the table that follows.

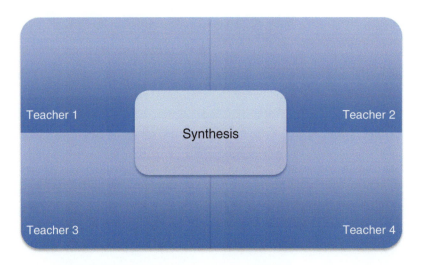

CLASS DISCUSSION
WITH GOALS AND CONTENT

Reasons Given
FOR METHODS AND MEDIA

Challenge

Control

Care

Confer

Captivate

Clarify

Consolidate

3.5 SPACE PLANNING

You have probably also had the experience of seeing how some classrooms shine because they are lovingly furnished and seem to be thought through to the smallest detail while other classrooms look drab and sober. In this respect, the question of effectiveness is crucial. Therefore, please answer the following questions: How often do you think about the planning of the room when preparing lessons? Is it the learners who design the room or is it you? Do you have certain strategies that, from your point of view, make room design effective for learning? In this chapter, we want to deal with this issue and consider, based on evidence, what needs to be taken into account when planning the room.

Many claims are made about the structure of schools and classrooms. Most countries are constantly building new schools, remodeling current ones, and renovating classrooms. In Munich, for example, learning houses with open spaces that facilitate open learning are promoted: "The Lying Classroom," the title of an article in the *Süddeutsche Zeitung* on April 29, 2019, is the future – children no longer have to sit at tables but can also learn lying down anywhere. A series of pictures of school classrooms from the 1900s through the 1950s and the 2000s often serves as an argument for these changes. Often there is the same picture: children sitting in rows, looking at the teacher and raising their hands. The message is clear: schools have not changed much.

There are many ideas about how innovative space design can support teaching and thereby improve learning outcomes. However, it must be noted that there is almost no evidence for all these ideas. Most of it is more wishful thinking than reality. One factor from the current Visible Learning dataset illustrates this: "Open vs. traditional classrooms" ($d = 0.02$).

Many see this factor as corresponding to the German concept of open instruction. This is incorrect. It is not for nothing that in Visible Learning, open classrooms are categorized under "Classroom." This factor primarily concerns structural changes. For example, what happens when traditional seating arrangements are replaced with group work tables, or when reading, working, and relaxation corners are set up in classrooms? Even though the empirical basis is older compared to other factors, the result, with an effect size of 0.02, is highly significant and clear: all these measures have no impact on students' academic performance because teachers do not automatically change their teaching style just because the external conditions have changed. They continue to teach according to their habits regardless of the spatial environment. However, if teachers embrace these new conditions and start to rethink their teaching, many innovations can enrich instruction.

As plausible as the ideas for learning spaces may be, they have little empirical support: surface structures, such as the arrangement of tables and chairs, do not have a decisive influence on learning success. The depth structures are much more important, such as how challenging the teaching is, the quality of the teacher–student relationship, and the type of error culture that prevails in the classroom.

Friedrich von Schiller (1856) sums up this idea in *The Parasite or the Art to Make One's Fortune* with the words: "There is room in the smallest hut for a happy loving couple." In other words, you can teach even under a tree effectively.

This is not to deny the importance of the room and its architecture, but to put it into perspective to the extent that the most beautiful room cannot do anything even with poor teaching. As important as the space and its architecture is, it is a surface characteristic of teaching. The depth structures are decisive.

Given the lack of evidence regarding the impact of space on learning success, the planning of the room appears insignificant. The following elements of room design, which are often discussed in detail, should therefore be seen merely as prompts to engage with the design of the space. They can have a positive effect, but only when the teacher aligns their instruction with these changes and adopts new teaching methods (cf. Barrett et al., 2015; Imms & Mahat, 2022; Nitsche & Zierer, 2013; Kahlert et al., 2013).

Arrangement of tables and chairs: The imagination with regard to possible seating arrangements seems to have no limits: row arrangement, individual tables, group tables, horseshoe shape, comb shape, and much more. All these possibilities have advantages and disadvantages and must be reflected against the background of spatial requirements, class situation, methodological considerations, and teaching personality.

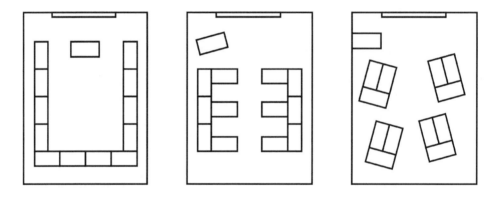

Figure 3.7

Furniture: As classrooms have to fulfill more and more functions, the furniture should also be adapted to the different requirements. Children of different ages (for example, from mixed classes or all-day classes) must be able to sit comfortably at the tables. This is possible if the table height is uniform and the chairs are equipped with a height-adjustable step surface. In addition, the students should have organization systems (cabinets, shelves, compartments, etc.) in which they can store their school supplies. In this way, the space is structured, work processes are structured, and the necessary order for the work is supported.

Color scheme: The color of a room could have a decisive influence on the atmosphere. Bright colors could make a room appear larger and friendly, while dark colors often seem oppressive. It is also possible to structure rooms and buildings with color. Thus, hallways, floors, or grades can be represented through certain colors and thus structure the building. Within a room, for example, corners can be given an explicit function through specific color design (e.g., writing corner, rest area, research workshop). Not only the color of the walls but also the color of the floor covering could be considered. But again, here the evidence is sparse and often missing.

Light and lighting: Classrooms toward the east and west can receive abundant daylight and have a low risk of glare. Oversized glazing has to be avoided, especially when the room is facing toward the sun's path for most of the year. Also, more electrical lighting with higher quality can provide a better visual environment.

Room acoustics: Several studies have shown that acoustic working conditions have a direct influence on learning (cf. Schiller et al., 2022). This characteristic, which also plays a decisive role in well-being in rooms, was previously paid little attention. Since teaching and learning is sometimes directly connected with verbal communication, this aspect is of particular importance, especially since many forms of cooperative work involve significantly more communication than a more monologue-based frontal lesson. Today, various types of absorbers (such as perforated panels, insulation boards, foam bodies) are applied to ceilings and walls in particular in order to optimize room acoustics, which has resulted in significant improvements, especially in large classrooms. Cost-effective alternatives (soft fiber boards as pin boards, curtains, carpets) also have an effect, but their effectiveness lags far behind structural measures. "Background music," which is repeatedly discussed in the context of acoustics, has no significant effect on learning performance ($d = 0.08$).

Air conditioning and ventilation: The term "climate" here is understood to mean the microclimate, i.e., the climatic conditions that prevail in the classroom and are thus largely influenced by humans. Although people perceive the temperature of a room very subjectively, studies have found that an optimal learning temperature is 21° C. In addition, care should be taken to ensure that the humidity is between 45 and 55 percent. Since the oxygen concentration in classrooms decreases quickly, attention must be paid to good ventilation. Shock ventilation is helpful, which involves opening all windows for a short time. A ventilation system can be installed in new buildings, which ensures permanent air exchange in the rooms.

Degree of structuring: Structuring is a key characteristic of effective teaching and can be enhanced through thoughtful spatial design. A well-organized space positively influences teaching, learning, and social interactions. Important considerations include: Can all students easily access their designated places? Are there areas for group activities (e.g., a seating circle, a semicircle in front of the table)? Is there a reading or experiment corner? Do students know where to find worksheet slots or the control station for station work? Clear and well-founded answers to these and similar questions streamline the teaching process. The more transparent and well-defined the room structure is for both students and teachers, the easier it is to achieve independent navigation and orientation.

Degree of co-design: The classroom is a communal living space and thus differs fundamentally from individually configurable space. Therefore, the interior design cannot meet all the wishes of the children. However, individual needs (e.g., seating in the vicinity of the whiteboard or smartboard because of a visual or auditory impairment, widening of traffic areas in the class because of a wheelchair user, economical decoration because of an ADHD student) must be taken into account. The establishment and design of classrooms are joint tasks that can be planned and carried out in a collaborative project or can be done successively over the entire school year. Participation in the room design increases identification with the designed room and the willingness to take responsibility. Participation can also have a preventive effect against disorder and vandalism.

In summary, it can be said that there are various possibilities to adapt school rooms to their respective functions and requirements and to design them according to pedagogical criteria. It should be borne in mind that school rooms must become identification spaces. Wherever possible, it makes sense to involve students and parents in the planning and implementation (participation). If students are given the opportunity to help with the design of school courses, the school garden, painting the walls, planning the classroom or cleaning it, their sense of responsibility for the classrooms and their furnishings will increase.

As important as these points are, regarding learning performance, the crucial point is that the design of the space alone is not effective. It always depends on how the teaching is conducted. High-quality instruction can benefit from well-thought-out spatial design, but high-quality instruction is not a result of the design alone.

One final point to address in the context of room planning is who sits and learns next to whom in the classroom. For this purpose, the analysis of the learners focuses on the fields of prior knowledge, learning behavior and working behavior, as well as social behavior. These can be taken up in the seating arrangement and guide action:

1. It is recommended to use the power of peers ("Strong classroom cohesion," $d = 0.66$; "Seeking help from peers," $d = 0.68$) and to form groups in which different performance levels are represented – moving from surface to deep to transfer. The basics for this have already been laid in section 3.1 on the decision area of the goals.
2. In order to counter the danger that only the stronger-performing students do the work, it is advisable to first distribute tasks in the group, so that every child has something to do (for example, the distribution of tasks in the group: writer, presenter, fetcher, and cleaner), and second, through differentiation, to ensure the performance levels fit with the leading goals (see factor bundles regarding goals with effect sizes of greater than $d = 0.4$). The latter have already been addressed in the section 3.1 on goal planning and section 3.2 on content planning.
3. Finally, it is recommended to not place learners who have a social behavior that needs to be developed with children with similar difficulties and place them as close to the teacher's location as possible. Here, too, the power of peers and learning can be used in the model ("Strong classroom cohesion," $d = 0.66$).

In view of the research findings on these factors, it is not recommended to use many different learning goals as a starting point for teaching. This is because it would result in many learning paths, which is not affordable for teachers in every-day school life. It would also result in the so-called scissor effect, where learners drift more and more apart in their performance and common learning becomes increasingly difficult.

As can be seen from the seating plan below, which we provide for illustration, an attempt was made to have a strong learner in each group, while children with poor learning performance, difficulties in learning and working methods, and challenges in social behavior were distributed among the groups.

Figure 3.8

Seating plans can be easily created in Excel – once a template has been created, changes can be made quickly. There are now also digital tools that can make this task easier (e.g., www.sitzplangenerator.de).

Undoubtedly, the same restriction applies to the seating plan as to the formulation of the goals: it is far from perfect. Rather, it has the potential to initiate discussions. That is exactly what we want to achieve – to get teachers to critically and constructively question their actions, to illuminate their habits, and to use evidence to think differently.

Exercises

Surface level

1. Go through the seating plan we presented above and discuss what you would do differently. What could be done differently?

Deep level

2. Take the analysis of the learners that you created with colleagues. Based on performance levels, learning and working methods, as well as social behavior, think about who would be best sitting next to whom. Reasons given could include that you always make decisions based on the quality of teaching, for example the 7 C's. At the end of the exercise, create a seating plan and transfer it to the following template.

Your classroom

3.6 TIME PLANNING

You have probably also had this experience: time cannot always be kept, teaching prompts do not always work, and you do not always end up exactly where you intended. Time eludes thorough planning. Hence, is it better to do without it altogether? What can an effective relationship with the planning of time look like? Which strategies are helpful to plan learning time for students sensibly? Experience shows that opinions on these questions differ widely among teachers, which is why you should reflect for yourself: Why is this question important or unimportant to me? In this section, we want to deal with this issue and consider, based on evidence, what needs to be taken into account when planning time.

The question of how to design a lesson in terms of timing can be primarily answered using two factors from "Visible Learning": "Lesson design" and "Direct instruction." Both factors have high effectiveness, with effect sizes of 0.70 and 0.56, respectively, making a detailed examination worthwhile.

The factor "Direct instruction" shows in a special way the combination of teaching quality on the one hand and the timing of the lessons on the other. With an effect size of 0.56, it is above the turning point. There are many myths surrounding the factor "Direct instruction," so one should take a closer look at it too.

These myths are due to a translation error, which equates direct instruction with teacher talk, scripted lessons, and a focus on facts. Even if a well-made teacher-centered lesson has many elements of direct instruction, they are two different methods with different development backgrounds.

Direct instruction is an approach that has been developed and continues to be refined within the field of instructional design. Today, there are several models whose common aspects include the following:

1. Clarity of goals on the part of the teacher
2. Clarity with regard to learning success on the part of the learners
3. Agreement on the goals and success of learning between learners and the teacher
4. Clarity with regard to methods and media use on the part of the teacher
5. Visualization of learning success
6. Exchange of lessons between learners and teacher
7. Continuation of the learning process

The difference from many forms of direct teaching is shown here as well as the meaning of dialogue. In order to produce clarity with regard to goals, content, methods, and media for both the teacher and learners, it is not only clarity on the part of the teacher that is needed. Above all, intensive phases of exchange, cooperation, and debate are important. This requires direct instruction, which when successful leads to corresponding clarity on the part of the learners.

Direct instruction thus describes a lesson in which both the teacher and learners know exactly who has to do what, when, why, how, where, and with whom. Like a director, the teacher leads the classroom in a didactically skillful way, without disregarding the activity of the students. Last but not least, students with poor learning skills benefit from this form of teaching, as they are more dependent on transparency, clarity of goals, and explicit teaching about the strategies of learning.

The term "lesson design" encompasses models that structure teaching from a temporal perspective based on pedagogical and didactic criteria. There are now numerous models, also called "learning cycle models," which may consist of three, four, five, or seven phases.

3E	4E	5E	7E
Explore	Engage	Engage	Elicit
		Explore	Engage
	Explore	Explain	Explore
Explain	Explain	Elaborate	Explain Elaborate Evaluate
Evaluate	Evaluate	Evaluate	Extend

The factor "Lesson design" has a high effect size of 0.70. This effectiveness is not dependent on the age of the learners, the subject taught, or the type of school. Comparing different models reveals a "golden mean" regarding the number of phases, where models with five phases achieve better effects than those with three, four, or seven phases. However, more important than the number of phases is the pedagogical and didactic coherence. Many commonalities are observed here, including student activation, lesson objectives, reinforcement of learning, and reflection on the learning process.

The following describes the 5E model in more detail:

Engage: At the beginning of a lesson, it is important to create an atmosphere conducive to learning. Teaching is essentially relationship work ("Teacher–student relationship," $d = 0.62$). Rules and rituals, such as greetings, can be helpful to build up a corresponding teaching and learning climate. In addition, clarity regarding central didactic categories should be achieved in this phase of the teaching ("Teacher clarity," $d = 0.85$). It can be seen, for example, in the fact that all participants in the teaching process know what the goal of the lesson is, what content is to be worked on, which methods are to be applied, and which media are available. It is nice to observe this clarity in the classroom when teachers manage to design a lesson entry in such a way that the learners formulate the lesson objective, which is then displayed on the blackboard or smartboard.

Explore: The connection to students' learning and performance level is a central aspect of successful teaching. Research results from neuropsychology show that the more possible it is to activate prior knowledge of learning, the more immediate and sustainable the learning is. One of the biggest challenges for teachers is to make prior knowledge of the learning visible in order to be able to build on it ("Piagetian levels," $d = 1.28$). It is obvious that an exercise on what has already been learned involves repeating the content – mostly at the levels of reproduction and reorganization. It is not only important to include this exercise in the lessons but also to talk to the learners about it ("Meta-cognition strategies," = 0.52).

Explain: The discussion of prior knowledge shows where additional knowledge is necessary in order to be able to answer the teaching question. Often individual learning steps that mark central enabling objectives result from student conjecture. In this respect, an information phase is necessary, which can be either externally controlled through the teacher or self-controlled through the learners. In both cases, effort and perseverance will be required to unlock the new content. In terms of method, the imagination has hardly any limits, encompassing the broad spectrum of working and action forms as well as social forms. For example, "Classroom discussion" ($d = 0.82$), "Concept mapping" ($d = 0.62$), "Direct instruction" ($d = 0.56$), and "Cooperative learning" ($d = 0.53$) are worth highlighting due to the effect sizes determined so far. Decisive for the choice of the method in this context is not the method itself but whether the method is suitable for achieving the set goal or not. The latter can always be seen in dependence on the initial learning situation and formulated in such a way that the learners can barely achieve it ("Appropriately challenging goals," $d = 0.60$).

Elaborate: After the students have worked out the leading goal with its specific goals, it is necessary to ensure knowledge gain. For this, a visualization of learning success is essential. External assessment through the teacher alone is often not correct, and may lack precision. It is not uncommon to observe that teachers consider their teaching to have been very successful, whereas learners have been endlessly bored with it – evidence based instead of dubious external assessment is the motto. One of the most promising ways to achieve this is a phase of deliberate exercise in which what is learned is processed. Feedback on the learning and performance level is again important.

Evaluate: The goal of school education is to cultivate independent learners, with students as authors of their own lives, as formulated by Julian Nida-Rümelin (2013). In this respect, an appraisal phase serves as the conclusion of a didactically thoughtful lesson, addressing two key aspects. First, it is important to carefully foster self-reflection on one's own learning and thus self-regulation ("Meta-cognition strategies," $d = 0.52$). Feedback questions can provide an orientation ("Feedback," $d = 0.51$): What did I do well and what did I do badly? Where did I make mistakes? How could I use these mistakes? What do I still have to work on? The latter question opens up the second aspect: learning is not finished with the end of the lesson. In particular, meaningful "Homework" ($d = 0.29$) is appropriate to ensure the sustainable learning success of the lessons and to deepen it. Forms of homework, which resemble deliberate practice, are preferable to undeliberate swotting. As a result, learners must be challenged, regularly and in a variety of ways.

Based on the findings of empirical educational research on the effectiveness of direct instruction and lesson design, the following four points can be recommended:

1. Structure your teaching into distinct phases from a temporal perspective – not too many and not too few; currently, five phases appear to be most effective.
2. Provide each phase with a clear pedagogical and didactic message, based on empirically validated models.
3. Base your articulation on a circular model so that the end of one lesson is always linked to the beginning of the next, providing a starting point for the subsequent lesson.
4. Make the phases of the lesson transparent and communicate them clearly so that students understand why the lesson is structured in this way. The clarity of the lesson is a result of the teacher's clarity, which becomes the students' clarity.

The above points apply to all described procedures for the planning of time and thus all of them share a common insight: planning of time does not take place for the sake of time itself. Rather, it is always basic pedagogical considerations that guide the classification of time – whether it is the awakening of interest, activation of prior knowledge, visualization of success criteria, or securing what has been learned. Teaching professionalism, and in this respect a certain understanding of teaching quality, thus forms the basis for the decision-making field of time. Against this background, the 7 C's should be mentioned again, which summarize pointedly evidence-based criteria for teaching quality.

As a consequence, this view has the outcome that the effectiveness of timing is more important than timekeeping. However, this does not mean that the effort to keep to time is unimportant; quite the opposite: in order to maintain attention and stay focused on the main thread, it is essential. However, if it becomes apparent in the classroom that the time allocation has been misjudged, such as when learners are overstretched, it is necessary to adjust the planned time allocation and react flexibly in the classroom. In the sense of an evidence-based didactics, it is crucial to take teaching quality criteria as the basis for this flexibility. Friedrich Copei (1962) underlined this point in terms of the fruitful moment.

If we integrate these considerations into the planning matrix, it is advisable to add an additional column for time management. Here, not only minutes should be recorded but also the instructional phases, such as those in the 5E model. This column can either stand independently or be linked with another column. The "Goals" column is particularly suitable for this purpose, as it sets the direction for the planning.

Exercises

Surface level

1. Outline the essential steps in the planning of time.

Deep level

2. Supplement your planning matrix with considerations for the time structure of a lesson. Plan these steps with colleagues and consider for each phase why it is important in class and how it can be implemented. Use a placemat again as a stimulus for the exchange. Each group member first thinks about how they would plan the time structure of the lesson and makes a suggestion on the sheet. The group members then read the suggestions on their own before the group comes together for an exchange of ideas. At the end of the exercise, an agreement is noted in the middle of the sheet and used for further planning. Transfer the results obtained in each case into the tables in the appendix for engage, explore, explain, elaborate, and evaluate.

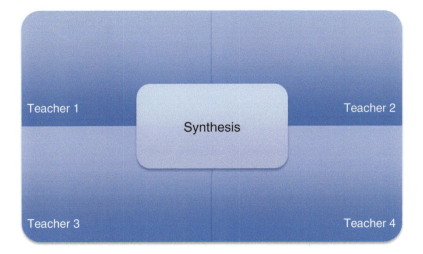

CHAPTER

Implementation

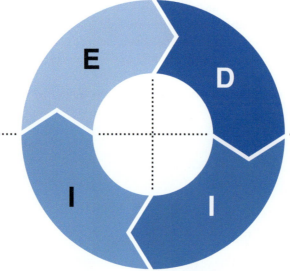

Evaluation—knowing the skills, having multiple methods, and collaboratively debating the magnitude of impact from the intervention.

Diagnosis and Discovery—using various assessment strategies to understand what each student brings to the lesson, including prior knowledge, motivations, and willingness to learn.

Implementation—a deep knowledge and understanding of the practices required to implement anything well.

Intervention—having multiple interventions such that if one does not work with the student the teacher changes to another intervention. In addition to knowing high-probability interventions, it is knowing when to adapt and apply thoughtful design in planning for learning.

Figure 4.1

The aims of this chapter
Once you have read and worked on this chapter, you should …

Surface level: Know that
- some aspects are important when implementing a teaching–learning situation.
- dialogue-based speech is characterized by conversational tone, mutual engagement and listening skills.

- prevention is better than intervention.
- different classroom management strategies are available.
- some aspects of a teaching–learning situation are conducive to an intact teacher–student relationship.

Deep level: Understand how
- to explain why a positive classroom climate allows for learners' mistakes to be seen as opportunities and not sources of embarrassment.
- to explain to what extent situational changes have to be taken into account when implementing a teaching–learning situation.
- to react both preventively and didactically to possible unscheduled events.
- to convert the goals, content, methods, media, room, and time decisions into a planning script.
- to reflect on whether your strengths and weaknesses can be seen with regard to the implementation of a teaching–learning situation.

The success criteria of this chapter

In order to be able to achieve the stated goals, it is necessary to understand the following content:

1. The Dialogue Promotors: dialogue-based talking in the class
2. The Controllers: classroom management
3. The Confidence Builders: strengthening of the teacher–student relationship in the lesson

As important and influential as thorough planning for learning success may be, it remains ineffective if the implementation is unsuccessful. There is not a linear relationship between planning success and learning success. In this respect, a number of aspects must be considered when carrying out the lesson. Since the planning of the lesson provides the basis for this, decisions have to be made on a case-by-case basis. Nevertheless, the results from Visible Learning indicate that at least the following three aspects are of general relevance.

First, research results repeatedly show that the teacher's share of speech is too great and often follows a mechanical imparting of knowledge in an error-oriented conversation. In Chapter 3, the context of method selection dealt with the factor bundle "The Dialogue Promotors" (e.g., "Collaborative learning," $d = 0.45$; "Decreasing disruptive behavior," $d = 0.82$; "Strong classroom cohesion," $d = 0.66$; "Peer- and self-grading," $d = 0.54$). This will be returned to once again within the context of implementation.

Second, empirical pedagogical research shows that there is no doubt that teaching is essentially based on relationships. In Chapter 3, the most important factors for this were summarized within the "Confidence Builder" bundle (e.g., "Teacher clarity," $d = 0.85$; "Teacher credibility," $d = 1.09$; "Teacher estimates of achievement," $d = 1.29$; "Teacher expectations," $d = 0.58$). In the context of implementation they have to be mentioned again.

Third, the implementation of lesson planning is supported by effective rules and rituals. The evidence for this statement can be found in the domain "Classroom" and has already been addressed in the context of the analysis of the learners but will now be viewed from a different perspective. From the perspective of implementation, the following factors demonstrate the importance of this research, which is summarized under the term "The Controllers" (e.g., "Classroom management," $d = 0.44$; "Decreasing disruptive behavior," $d = 0.82$).

In essence, three sets of factors and thus fields of action are marked that are so important in the context of the implementation of teaching that they must always be a part of lesson planning – regardless of whether the teacher is a novice or expert, the class is known or unknown, or the learners' performance is strong or weak.

Figure 4.2

Regarding the bundle of factors "The Dialogue Promotors," it is a recurring requirement not to teach from the teacher's point of view in the form of a monologue. While there is hardly a teacher who would disagree with this requirement, the degree of approval drops when it comes to your own teaching. Many teachers claim they talk a lot, and when probed on this the typical response is that they talk for about 40 percent of the time. Does this sound like you? The empirical results are helpful but show a much higher percentage of time. For example, Helmke et al. (2008, cf. Hattie, 2023) show that self-assessments of the teacher's share of speech in a lesson deviates significantly from the actual measured time. On average, teachers dominate the classroom talk – about 90 percent of the time it is the teacher talking and 10 percent the students.

A typical pattern can be identified in the analysis of teachers' speech in the classroom. After a long input phase, the teacher formulates a question that they ask the class. Then a learner is called and asked for an answer. Finally, the teacher evaluates the response, continuing with a longer input phase until the next question is asked. This pattern, known as IRE, which stands for "initiation," "response," and "appraisal," does not meet any of the criteria mentioned above of teaching quality, as explained with the help of the 7 C's: challenges are not set because the dialogues focus on surface understanding and mostly only factual knowledge is

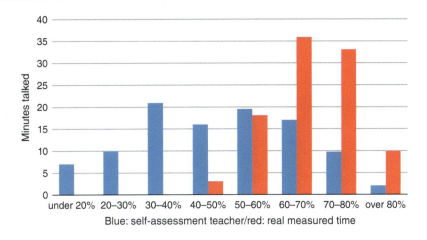

Figure 4.3

requested; errors in the learning process are not used for learning because they are not followed up (the errors are corrected by the teacher or by another learner); metacognitive strategies are disregarded because the learning processes are not made visible; the power of peers is not taken into account; and finally there is a lack of appreciation because learners do not perceive themselves as participants in learning but as an audience.

How is it that teachers still feel that their lessons are dialogue based and work? On the one hand, an important finding of Visible Learning must be pointed out, which is that 95 percent of what happens in the classroom positively affects students' learning performance. This is a very low standard, but it does mean teachers can "find evidence" from their practice that their monologues "improve" learning. Hence, students learn in a lesson that follows the pattern of "answering questions" or the IRE response method, which confirms what many teachers do. But students don't learn as much as they could learn if there was a better balance of monologue and dialogue. And this is the key. But there is a conspiracy: above-average students prefer the teacher to engage in monologue and focus on the facts – as that is a game in which they are the winners.

It is worth drawing on Bakhtin's (1981) distinction between "monologue-based" and "dialogue-based" speech. It is not about teachers simply reducing their amount of speech; rather, the nature of dialogue in the classroom needs to be different. What is needed is more student talk, many more student questions, seeing errors as opportunities to learn and relearn, thinking aloud about how to solve problems and dilemmas, talking about how to evaluate knowledge and ideas, and seeking, providing, and interpreting feedback. Learners do not need less of what they already receive but something else. This "dialogue-based" speech enables the realization of the quality criteria of the lessons in a special way, by setting a challenge that activates learners, ensures smooth lessons, ensures an appreciative atmosphere, arouses relevant motivation, clearly communicates instructions, and ensures long-term learning success – and with that, the 7 C's are once again given as justification.

The key to this "dialogue-based" speech are questions and consequently the listening skills of the teacher. Beginners in particular find it difficult to hold back and wait. The simplest and most effective of all questions is one toddlers ask us every day: "Why?" As exhausting as this question may be in everyday life with toddlers, it forces adults to think, question what is self-evident, and reformulate what has been said. This is ultimately what makes peers so powerful in the learning process: they recap and examine what has been said, they question and recall, they repeat and supplement, and they exhort and encourage both students and the teacher to explain something again (cf. Mercer & Littleton, 2007). Hence, it is important to use the question of *why* again and again and to initiate conversations in the classroom. Sadly, within a few years of starting school this early love of the *why* question (indicating that the child is trying to build a theory of their world and engage in curious inquiry) switches to *what* questions as they come to believe that "knowing lots" is the aim of the game.

Against this background, a second strategy stands out for the realization of "dialogue-based" speech in the classroom: mistakes. At its core, learning means making mistakes (and in teaching, by the way, too). Every mistake that often occurs in the classroom opens the opportunity to take a closer look and make the thinking visible. In doing so, misunderstandings are pronounced and discrepancies named. Hence, it is important to use mistakes in the learning process again and again to get into a conversation about learning. Students continually make mistakes, so it should be a normal, not embarrassing, process to identify, discuss, and evaluate them. Develop a culture of errors in which the learners are not afraid of errors but welcome them and use them as an occasion for mutual exchange: "Why is that not correct? Please explain it to me again!" If learners make such statements on their own initiative, then you have done a lot in the direction of a positive error culture. If a class has reached this stage, then a board with the heading "Mistakes of the Week," for example, can be a clear signal to everyone that learners are encouraged to make what they did not understand visible, with everyone invited to contribute to solving the problems. Ultimately, many methods can be used to implement more dialogue in the class: group discussions, group puzzles, fishbowl, placemat activities, etc.

Regarding the factor bundle "The Controllers," young professionals are often plagued by self-doubt if the lesson that they have painstakingly planned does not go as it should. Particularly stressful are those lessons in which teaching and learning comes to a standstill or even stops completely because students deliberately or unintentionally disturb their planning. Experienced teachers have often found methods for such situations that they can use successfully (e.g., switching to an alternative teaching strategy, moving to more complex material). However, young professionals may not have developed such adaptive flexibility.

In this context Jacob S. Kounin's (2006) research is ground-breaking: in his studies he has shown that preventon is better than any reprimand. He developed various criteria of classroom management. These criteria are not to be seen as recipes – they are too general and far too abstract. Rather, they are to be understood as a reflection tool, helping teachers to take a critical, constructive view of their own teaching. In the planning matrix, these questions are supplemented accordingly in the "Control" area:

- Omnipresence and overlapping: Try to signal to the students that you are present in the classroom and you notice little things. Do not respond to any disruption immediately with your full attention (as this can lead to escalation).
- Smoothness and momentum: Avoid loss of speed and idling in your lessons, as these particularly provoke students' digression as well as reducing effective teaching and learning time. This requires a series of rules and rituals, forms of work and patterns of action that must be worked out together with the students. For example, in the classroom, divide up the tasks among the group in the lesson beforehand, so that there are no delays to the actual smooth running of the lesson.
- Maintaining group focus: Try to address all students at the same time as often as possible, or if you need to speak to a group in more detail, keep the other students busy with an assignment.
- Avoiding weariness: Classroom disruptions can usually be avoided if the lesson is experienced as stimulating, varied, profitable, and joyful. Therefore, ensure successful outcomes by avoiding situations that may lead to offense, undue exposure, or excessive demands. Thus, weaker learners receive support so that they can achieve the learning objective, while stronger learners receive less support so that they can also achieve the common learning objective.

It may also be necessary to have a small repertoire of action patterns in order to be able to react quickly and in a versatile manner to disorder. Against the background of the preventive measures, the following points apply:

- Non-verbal interventions are preferable.
- Early intervention is needed.
- Positive reinforcement is better than warning and punishment.

The following intervention measures are to be understood accordingly. Let's take the example of a student who snaps their fingers very loudly when raising their hand, causing disruption in the classroom.

- Deliberately ignoring: You continue with the lesson and do not immediately address the classroom disruption. Many students will refrain from further disturbance actions if they realize that the teacher is not paying them the attention they hoped for.

- Rewarding: After ignoring them the first time, praise the student the next moment they behave according to the rules and your expectations.
- Giving signs: You continue with the lesson, pointing at or making eye contact with the disruptive student as a symbol for calm and quiet in the classroom. This emphatic and indirect admonition is often sufficient to prevent further disruption.
- Reducing the physical distance: You continue with the lesson, but approach the disruptive student. Due to physical proximity, the student's courage to continue disrupting the lessons often disappears. Or alternatively, move further away, and the lack of attention may also suffice.
- Showing humor: You briefly interrupt your class and respond to the classroom disorder with humor before continuing with the class. For example, you could reply to a student who snaps their fingers very loudly when raising their hand: "Thomas is extremely motivated today. Are your fingers still intact?" The laughter should be on your side.
- Activation of the disruptive student: You use the class disruption and take on the disruptive student immediately by involving them in the further course of the class. For example, you could say to the student who is snapping their fingers: "Thomas has put his hand up. What do you think, Thomas?" If the disruptive student does not know the answer, they will likely reconsider disrupting the class again.
- Regrouping of the students: In the case of long-lasting class disturbances caused by individual or several students, it can make sense to change the seating arrangement and, above all, to position those causing the disruption in such a way that they are far enough apart and also within reach.

In terms of the factor bundle "The Confidence Builders," the idea that teaching is essentially a relationship can be found since the beginning of discussions about teaching. It is thus not surprising that the factor "Teacher–pupil relationship" in Visible Learning achieves an effect size of 0.63 and is therefore one of the more effective factors. The following three examples are intended to illustrate how teachers in the phase of implementation can implement these results in a specific way.

1. Consider the concept of "not yet": this is one of the simplest study designs in psychological research and is based on a study by Carol Dweck (2012). Dweck investigated what influence teachers saying to learners "You can't do this" had on them, compared to "You can't yet." While the first statement demotivates, frustrates, and stigmatizes learners, the second statement leads to a level of confidence, commitment, and performance improvement. Why? "Not yet" signals to the learners that they can reach the goal if they make an effort or engage in learning, that they are on the right path, that it is worth

moving on, and that increased effort can be rewarded with success if they continue to work.
2. The IKEA effect: Even if you do not know this effect, you certainly will know IKEA (cf. Hattie & Yates, 2015, p. 295f.). And you may have had the experience that it is not so easy to assemble shelving from the thousands of parts you get when you make your purchase. Economic psychology studies found that people who succeed in doing so place a much higher value on the IKEA shelving than on an expensive antiquarian item. How does this difference come about? It is due to the effort and commitment that had to be put in to form a whole from the individual parts. This effort and commitment go directly into the product, remain in the memory, and lead to an increase in value. What are the consequences for school and teaching? Whenever a learner works on something with effort and commitment, it is the teacher's duty to show appreciation and respect for the learners' performance. By teachers doing this, it will result in a strengthening of the teacher–student relationship. Failure to do so may result in a breakdown in the teacher–student relationship.
3. "Send a smile on the journey": It is not a ground-breaking realization that joy and well-being are essential components of successful teaching and benefit the learning process. This is not to say that the role of the teacher is to make learners constantly laugh or to mutate into clowns themselves. But it is still necessary that, with all the required seriousness, learning must also enable phases of laughter, manifest enjoyment, and pleasure about teaching and learning. Psychologically speaking, teachers have a trump card in their hands. Smiling is contagious – especially when it comes from the heart – is honest and authentic, and is shared with the community. A study was carried out on this phenomenon in the 1990s (cf. Hattie & Yates, 2013, p. 250, et seq.). In the pedestrian zones of large cities, the experimenter smiled at strangers. The result was that more than half of the passersby smiled back automatically. Hence, it is up to teachers whether there is laughter in the classroom or not and whether humor and joy find their way into it. Reactions as simple as smiling send positive signals that enhance the relationship, while negative signals can occur as a consequence of not smiling.

In conclusion, our advice is to do it like a top athlete before a big competition. Mentally rehearse your lesson in your mind (or in the classroom without learners). This creates a "film in the head." In this way, planning weaknesses are brought to mind and you get to know yourself better as an actor. In addition, be your own "Devil's Advocate" – evaluating your lesson planning and looking for strengths and weaknesses, as well as opportunities and threats.

Exercises

Surface level

1. Reflect on the following questions about your planning by mentally working through your lesson:

    At which point of the lesson are *why* questions necessary?
    When can errors occur that are important for the learning process and the achievement of goals?
    Where can malfunctions occur that can be avoided preventively?
    Where can disturbances arise for which an intervention will be necessary?

Deep level

2. Rehearse your lesson planning with a colleague in an empty classroom and watch how you act, where you have your strengths and where your weaknesses are. If necessary and if possible, record individual passages on video. Together think about how you can optimize your lesson planning.

CHAPTER 5

Evaluation

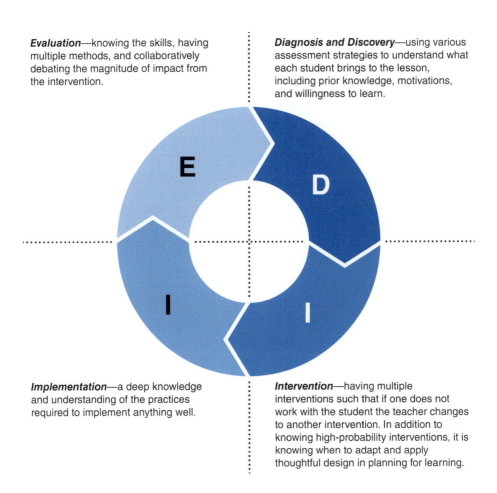

Figure 5.1

"Why should I worry about a lesson afterward? Learners have none of it, and I rack my brains unnecessarily." "I know best what went well and what went wrong. I don't need the students for that." "I don't have to evaluate my lessons. The learners have to evaluate themselves." Have you met these statements before, or do you think about the evaluation of teaching–learning situations? In this chapter, we want to examine these opinions critically and constructively.

The aims of this chapter

Once you have read and worked on this chapter, you should …

Surface level: Know that

- specific aspects are important when assessing a teaching–learning situation.
- feedback, evaluation, and summative and formative feedback result in different types of understanding.
- there are different feedback levels.
- there are different feedback perspectives.
- different methods can used for effective evaluation of a lesson.

Deep level: Understand how

- to comment on the extent to which summative and formative feedback must be considered when assessing a teaching–learning situation.
- to explain under which aspects feedback can be effective.
- to give reasons why feedback levels and feedback perspectives are related.
- to explain why evidence-based evaluation is important when assessing a teaching–learning situation.
- to have strategies to effectively integrate homework into the classroom.
- to reflect on whether your strengths and weaknesses can be seen with regard to the evaluation of a teaching–learning situation.

The success criteria of this chapter

In order to be able to achieve the stated goals, it is necessary to understand the following content:

1. Definitions: Feedback, evaluation, and summative and formative feedback
2. Formative feedback
3. Feedback levels
4. Feedback perspectives
5. Summative feedback
6. Homework, quiz etc.
7. Evidence-based method variety

You may know the slogan: "A game lasts 90 minutes." And "After the game is before the game." They come from Sepp Herberger, one of the most successful and well-known soccer coaches of all time. In 1954 he led Germany to the World Cup with a victory over the Hungarians, who were considered unbeatable at the time: the miracle of Bern. At first glance, both sayings seem trivial. At second glance, however, they indicate an essential basic understanding of performance and success: it always depends on how a game develops and what conclusions are drawn from a game. In other words: know thy impact!

This addresses the central attitude of successful teachers, who see themselves as evaluators of their own teaching. In this respect, evaluation of the teaching–learning situation becomes both the first and final step of lesson preparation, in addition to the phases of analysis, planning, and implementation. Once again, in conversations with teachers, there is an understanding of the importance of this phase. Too often, only the implementation phase takes place in everyday school life and there is too little focus on the impact of the implementation. The reassurance of having also addressed this aspect of impact usually does not last long, quickly giving way to the feeling that learners have not understood anything and the pace was too fast. It is then laborious to go back in the learning process and explain concepts step by step from the beginning – if the time is available and the teacher decides to do this.

The empirical evidence for the importance of the evaluation phase of the teaching–learning process is more visible than in any other phase. The following set of factors, summarized under the term "The Evaluator," is intended to clarify what has been said:

Factor	d
Practice testing	0.49
Formative evaluation	0.40
Alternative assessment methods	0.64
Feedback	0.51
Mastery learning	0.67
Evaluation and reflection	0.75
Response to intervention	0.73

What key messages can be drawn from this table? First, it is striking that the factors mentioned all show effect sizes above the hinge point and therefore have an above-average positive effect. Second, it shows that the connection to the goals of the lesson is an essential feature of the factors. It is the guarantee of the high effects. Third, the various procedures make it clear that the evaluation of the teaching–learning situation starts at different points, essentially during the lesson as well as at the end of the lesson. And fourth, it becomes apparent that successful evaluation of the teaching–learning process relies on an exchange between the learners and teacher. Evaluation is not a one-way street but a dialogue. Evaluation is not reflection; it is a critique of teacher and student reflection.

For teachers in general and daily lesson preparation in particular, it follows that the broad field of evaluative thinking is a central component of successful lesson planning. But what can evaluation and evaluative thinking mean?

Michael Scriven (1967) distinguishes formative and summative evaluation. A formative evaluation is carried out in the course of the implementation of an intervention and the data obtained from it can thus be further processed to improve the impact of the learning, whereas a summative evaluation is located at the end of the intervention and can thus be seen as its conclusion. Note that he never used the misleading terms formative and summative assessment – any assessment can be used for formative or summative evaluation, and these terms focus too much on the assessments and not the use of the assessment information. It is obvious that formative and summative evaluation have different effects on students' learning performance. Results from a formative evaluation aim to be immediately fruitful for learners, whereas results from a summative evaluation are provided at the end of the learning, often when there is little opportunity to use the information for improvement. As Bob Stake quipped: When the cook tastes the soup it is formative; when the guests taste the soup, it is summative. They have different purposes and both can be valuable. It is therefore an essential part of lesson planning to consider aspects of formative and summative evaluation.

Figure 5.2

The corresponding procedures are summarized in Visible Learning under the factor "Feedback." It is worth noting that feedback is one of the best-researched methods: over 20 meta-analyses in the past 30 years with an average effect size of 0.51 have been identified. This breadth of research into feedback obscures how to determine successful feedback, which is not a trivial issue. In addition, teachers rightly answer "yes" to the question of whether they give a lot of feedback – indeed, they do..

But successful feedback is not a question of quantity; it is a question of quality. What is most critical is whether the feedback was heard, understood, and actioned. And the nature of the feedback, depending on the stage of the learning cycle, is equally critical. This is where the research in the context of Visible Learning (cf. also Hattie & Timperley, 2007) is particularly helpful, as it shows the associated differences. There are four feedback levels that can be used and they have different effects.

The four feedback levels

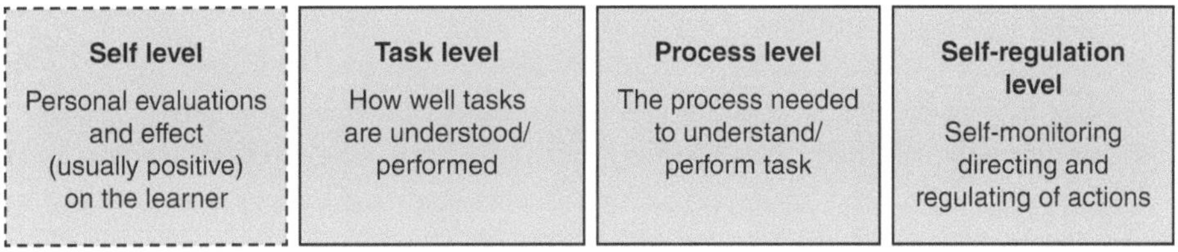

Self level	Task level	Process level	Self-regulation level
Personal evaluations and effect (usually positive) on the learner	How well tasks are understood/ performed	The process needed to understand/ perform task	Self-monitoring directing and regulating of actions

Figure 5.3

First, feedback at the level of the self includes all feedback that focuses on the personality or personal attributes of the recipient of the feedback. Praise, but also censure, in all its possible variants are examples – such as "You are great!", "You are wonderful!", "You are a hard-working student!" or "You are good!" However, the effects on learning performance are minor to negative – why is this? It is because feedback at the level of the self contains no information about the learning process but is almost exclusively associated with personality traits. Under certain circumstances, this can even have negative effects, as learners may interpret these forms of feedback as evaluations of themselves as individuals. Consequently, they may often feel that they are receiving praise for their personality traits and not for themselves as learners. They note that while the "learners" in the class receive feedback about their work, the feedback they receive is about themselves as individuals. If there is excessive praise, this can lead to a reduction in the willingness to perform because learners tend not to want to jeopardize their positive image constantly. In the same way, blame can lead to a negative self-concept because it is not directed toward the cause and the possible error, but rather towards the person. Feedback at the level of the self becomes particularly problematic if learners already have high intrinsic motivation because it then acts as a variant of extrinsic motivation. In the worst case, this results in learners' intrinsic motivation decreasing and their extrinsic motivation correspondingly increasing – and that is exactly what no teacher wants because the worse variant from a psychological perspective is an extrinsically motivated learner.

Feedback is more effective and sustainable if learners have a high level of intrinsic motivation and at the same time a low level of extrinsic motivation. A prime example of this train of thought is the use of rewards (such as candy, sweets, stickers, stamps), which many teachers give to learners for orderly and disciplined work. However, sweets are not only unhealthy; from a pedagogical point of view they are also poison for fostering intrinsic motivation. The importance of feedback at the level of the self relates more to the teacher–student relationship, where it can have a positive effect. Praising effort and the person is often the essence of a good relationship. However, there are far more effective methods to create an atmosphere of security, trust, and confidence while developing positive relationships. There is a consensus in research to use feedback at the level of the self in carefully measured or very limited quantities and after careful consideration. Often "less is more" can be a guide.

Unlike feedback at the level of the self, which has been described as personality related, feedback at the levels of the task, processes, and self-regulation relate to the performance demonstrated by the learner. The effect of feedback on these levels can be seen more positively, but to varying degrees, as a closer analysis shows.

Second, feedback at the level of the task is understood as the feedback that learners receive with regard to their factual knowledge on the ideas or content of the lesson. For example, when completing a test of the main ideas in the lesson, students can receive feedback about whether their answers were correct or incorrect. This feedback is important as these main ideas can be critical to going deeper and engaging in problem-solving. Such feedback can point to their errors, resources for better understanding, and reteaching the ideas and content.

Third, feedback can be given at the level of processes, focusing on students' ways of thinking or choices of learning strategies. For example, a teacher who assigned a performance test can review the implementation or impact of the student learning processes. For example, if the test revealed quick work or over-speedy responses, this can be a sign of sloppiness, with many careless mistakes. In this case, the learner receives information about *how* they worked.

Fourth, feedback at the level of self-regulation occurs when teachers invite students to engage in error management, identify more optimal learning strategies, and take more responsibility in driving their own learning. This type of feedback is more about the processes used to assist students to become more engaged and successful in their learning. For example, after a performance test, the teacher can report back to the learners about how they managed to focus their attention during the test and used time management and self-controlling strategies. As a result, learners are able to gain clarity on how they regulated the product and process of their performance themselves.

Please reflect (or make a video) on a recent class. What feedback did you give? Try to classify it into the four levels of feedback, identifying what level was dominant. If your lesson was primarily vocabulary and knowledge development, then 80 percent should have been at the task level and 20 percent stretching the students to deeper understanding. If the lesson was primarily for students to learn at a deeper level, consolidate their understanding, or deliberately practice the ideas, then it should have been 80 percent process feedback and 20 percent stretching the students to take more responsibility in driving their learning (as well as feedback about errors or misconceptions about the ideas). If the lesson was primarily for students to engage in their own learning and growth, then 80 percent should have been to help them further drive their learning (and 20 percent about the [next] tasks and processes).

We have conducted a survey on this across many classes (cf. Sanders & Zierer, 2019). The result is always the same: the vast majority of students want feedback at the level of processes or self-regulation, while a few ask for feedback at the level of the task or processes. However, the majority of classes are dominated by task feedback. And there is a conspiracy: many above-average students prefer task feedback – as knowing lots is the game, they are winners. But this rarely advances their learning and achievement in the deeper, more relational aspects of lessons.

	What feedback do learners want? (Sanders & Zierer, 2019)	What feedback do learners get?			
		Hattie & Masters (2011)	Van den Bergh et al. (2010)	Gan (2011)	Sanders & Zierer (2019)
Task	17%	59%	51%	70%	85%
Process	23%	25%	42%	25%	10%
Self-regulation	48%	2%	2%	1%	1%
Self	12%	14%	5%	4%	14%

In this context, it finally becomes clear that successful feedback is not a question of quantity but of quality. What good is it for a learner, for example, if a mistake is made clear to them again and again but without giving them specific information on what is causing the error and how it can be worked on in the future? In other words, more feedback at the level of the task does not have far-reaching effects. Only when it is combined with feedback at the levels of the process and self-regulation can it develop its effect.

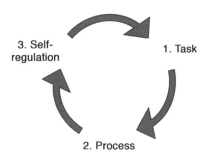

Figure 5.4

It would be wrong to give the impression at this point that one feedback level is better than another. Rather, the core message is that the different feedback levels interlock and work together, depending on where students are in the learning cycle. It is important to provide feedback at the levels of the task, process, and self-regulation.

The following questions serve to clarify the important feedback levels of the task, process, and self-regulation:

Task

- Does the student's answer meet the criteria for success?
- Is the answer right or wrong?
- How can the answer be formulated in more detail?
- What is the right answer and what is the wrong answer?
- What is missing so that the answer can be comprehensive?

Process

- Which strategies were used in the learning process?
- What went well in the learning process and what can be improved?
- Where are the strengths and where are the weaknesses to be seen in the learning process?
- What other information does the processing of the task contain with regard to the learning process?

Self-regulation

- What goals can the student indicate as being achieved?
- What are the reasons given by the student for having solved a task correctly or incorrectly?
- How does the student explain their success?
- What are the next goals and tasks?
- How can the student control and monitor their learning process themselves?

Against the background of the feedback levels, it is essential to reflect on how the weighting of the feedback levels depends on the performance level of the learners. Consider the following example:

In a series of lessons relatively new to the students, it is worth ensuring that they know the appropriate facts, contents, and ideas first – and here is where task feedback can be particularly powerful. Correcting errors, explaining misunderstandings, and reteaching concepts is what is most needed. As the lesson moves to making connections between the ideas and moving to deeper conceptual understanding, process feedback is powerful. This involves asking students to work with you to detect errors, try alternative learning strategies, and start to bring together and consolidate the seemingly many ideas. The final phase of the lesson could involve the students generalizing or transferring their knowledge and knowing to new ideas and situations, discovering how to relate their learning to other domains of their knowledge. This is where teachers need to gradually release their responsibility, invite students to teach each other, talk out loud about their thinking processes, and critique and provide each other with feedback.

Consequently, the higher the performance level of learners, the more feedback at the level of self-regulation is necessary, but this should *not* presume that lower-ability students do not receive process and regulation feedback as a normal part of the lesson. They should not be constrained to only learning the facts. Against this background, feedback emerges as a complex didactic tool for controlling and optimizing learning processes, which is related to other aspects of successful teaching.

In addition to the differentiation in feedback levels, each of these levels can be operated from three perspectives: "Feed Up," "Feed Back," and "Feed Forward."

- "Feed Up" or "Where am I going?" indicates feedback that compares the actual status with the current target status. Hence, it is related to the present and should therefore be defined as present-related feedback.
- "Feed Back" or "How am I going?" highlights feedback that compares the actual status with the previous actual status.
- "Feed Forward" or "Where to next?" describes feedback that explains the target status to be achieved based on the actual status. It is therefore directed toward the future and should therefore be defined as future-related feedback.

For example, the teacher can report back to the learners at the level of the task, first informing them about which tasks have been solved correctly and which ones incorrectly, which indicates their current status in comparison to the target status set ("Feed Up"). Second, the teacher can state how the current performance level of the learners has changed compared to the last performance test, including where it has improved and where it has not ("Feed Back"). Third, the teacher can provide information on which tasks are to be processed in the future and which future target state results from this ("Feed Forward").

Against this background, successful feedback can be seen from past, present, and future perspectives. All three build on one another and together form a comprehensive picture. It becomes clear that present-based feedback is based on past-related feedback and is itself to be seen as the forerunner of future-oriented feedback. Again and again, Visible Learning emphasizes that it is important for successful feedback to be as complete as possible. But what does complete feedback look like? Which areas need to be considered? How can the levels of feedback be combined with the perspectives of feedback? While the importance of feedback has gained increased recognition as a result of the reception to Visible Learning, gaining the attention it deserves, so many things remain unclear in practice. Therefore, an attempt is made below to consolidate the levels and perspectives of feedback into a feedback matrix and to fill it in with sample questions.

Visible Learning: Lesson Planning

	Levels of feedback			
		Task	**Process**	**Self-regulation**
Perspectives of feedback	Past ("Feed Back")	What progress has the learner made on goals and content?	What progress has the learner made on task completion? Is there evidence of Improvement?	What progress has the learner made on self-regulation strategies?
	Present ("Feed Up")	What goals did the learner reach? What content did the learner understand?	How did the learner complete the task? Is there evidence of how the learner worked?	What self-regulation strategies did the learner successfully apply?
	Future ("Feed Forward")	What goals should be set next? What content should be learned next?	What tips on task completion should the learner be given next?	What self-regulation strategies should the learner apply next?

This feedback matrix illustrates the complexity of feedback and the need for the professionalization of teachers. We have found that reducing it to the following three areas is helpful as a starting point because it takes into account all perspectives and all levels, but does not pick up on all possible combinations.

	Feedback levels			
		Task	**Process**	**Self-regulation**
Perspectives of feedback	Past ("Feed Back")		*Where is there progress in terms of performance? Are there indications of better processing?*	
	Present ("Feed Up")	*What goals were achieved? What content was understood?*		
	Future ("Feed Forward")			*What self-regulation strategies are to be applied next?*

The discussion about feedback is often dominated by the idea that it is directed from the teacher to the learners. As important as this form of the feedback is, it needs also to include feedback from the students to the teacher. The teacher cannot answer all of the questions as to whether the goals have been achieved, whether the content has been understood, whether the methods were useful, and whether the lesson materials were helpful. Only the learners are able to do this.

How often can it be seen that teachers leave the classroom satisfied because everything seems to have gone well, but the students only worked not in order to learn but to avoid sanctions, and in general just became bored? This strategy is called "Gaming the system."

Recall Nuthall's (2007) finding that teachers do not see or hear 80 percent of what occurs in the classroom. We need teachers to be listeners to what the students are saying, feeling, and hearing. Experience has shown that feedback takes courage because teachers are not prepared for some of the student feedback. It does not help that during teacher training, teachers are still socialized into being lone fighters, avoiding mistakes, and keeping the students busy.

A simple example is the feedback coordinate system. In this, two important aspects of the lesson can be recorded and worked on by the learners. Here is a completed example:

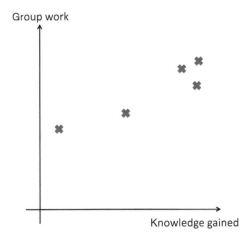

Figure 5.5

For example, if a learner is of the opinion that the group work went well and the knowledge gained was high, then they would put a cross in the top right. If, on the other hand, the student is of the opinion that the group work went badly and the knowledge gain was low, they would put a cross in the bottom left. This feedback can be obtained quickly. The feedback chart can be hung on the classroom door, with learners marking it when leaving the classroom. It only takes a few minutes but provides important information to the teacher.

Depending on the feedback given on the level of the learners, this procedure can be expanded. There is a wealth of other ideas in the literature. Here is an example of a feedback target that has not yet been filled: Students have to assess the quality of the lesson based on the given criteria (atmosphere, organization, etc.) and place a cross accordingly. The better they feel a criterion was met during the lesson, the closer toward the center they should place the cross.

Visible Learning: Lesson Planning

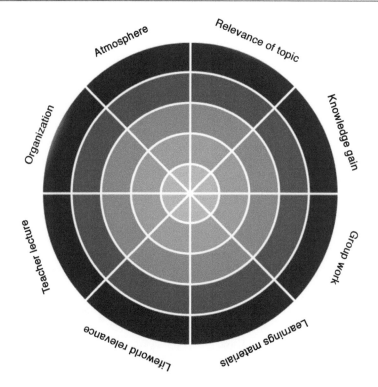

Figure 5.6

It has already been mentioned that how teachers deal with feedback from learners is a question of expertise. This is also made clear by the examples mentioned. At first glance, the students who work on a feedback coordinate system or a feedback target only give feedback at the level of tasks and processes and not at the level of self-regulation. In addition, in these cases they only provide feedback from the perspective of the present. However, the teacher can use this information to make a comparison to the past by putting earlier feedback next to it and creating future-related feedback from it. Likewise, from feedback at the level of the task, they can consider what consequences this has for the teaching process and their own self-regulation. This shows that feedback is not something set in stone. Feedback is the starting point for an endless dialogue. Giving feedback implies taking feedback and vice versa.

Not to be forgotten here are procedures with new media, such as computers and tablets. If used correctly, they can reveal knowledge that would be difficult or even impossible to make visible without them – again, this is evidence that new media are not a sure-fire success but need people to be effective. The advantage of new media in this context can be seen particularly in the fact that their use enables more complex feedback combined with a low workload.

The focus of the factor "Formative evaluation" is therefore comprehensive questionnaires that learners can fill out quickly and easily using software. The result is then available in a matter of seconds. The effectiveness of these methods is high, although the decisive factor is not the collection of the data but the evaluation. This confirms a principle of feedback: it is the ticket to dialogue, and the dialogue decides whether the feedback will take effect or not.

Here is an example of a type of digital feedback (cf. Zierer & Wisniewski, 2019) that was obtained with an app at the end of a lesson. The data in the overall evaluation with regard to a factor provided the following results:

Figure 5.7

The following figure shows a comparison of the perspectives of learners and the teacher (self-perception):

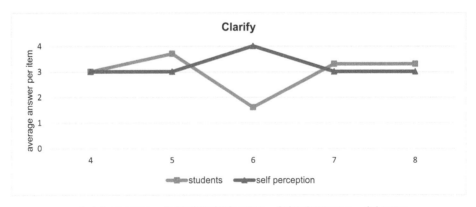

Figure 5.8

And the following figure shows a detailed evaluation of the learners (cf. Zierer & Wisniewski, 2019):

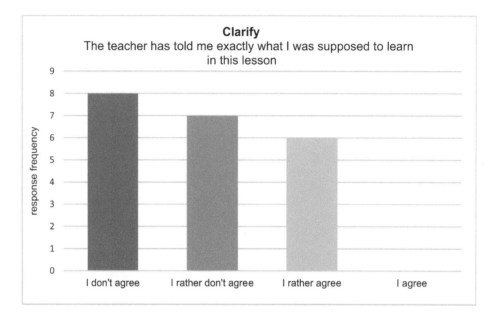

Figure 5.9

In the example shown, the conclusion drawn from the overview of the overall factors is that the "Clarify" factor, one of the 7 C's, represents a key development task that can be explored using a SWOT analysis. With regard to the individual items of this factor, it was found that Question 6 resulted in a particularly large deviation between the external assessment by the learners and the self-assessment by the teacher. In order to avoid outliers causing this difference, a detailed evaluation was taken into account. It was found that the majority of the class believed that there was no clear goal setting. In conversation with the learners, several points were discussed as to why students had this impression, and in exchange with colleagues, the teacher considered further strategies for the next lesson to create more clarity for the students.

In this context, the importance of using measures to obtain feedback at the end of the lesson cannot be overestimated. These measures make it possible to check in a short time whether the most important goals have been achieved and the central content has been understood, whether the selected methods are usable, and whether the media provided was useful. This feedback can be obtained through a simple crossword puzzle, a reflection in a learning diary, or the homework for the next lesson.

Exercises

Surface level

1. Outline essential steps in the evaluation of teaching–learning situations.

Deep level

2. Plan with colleagues the evaluation of your next few lessons. Create a feedback matrix and quiz for a key learning objective. Use the following placemat again as a stimulus for the exchange. Each group member first thinks for themselves how they would plan the evaluation of the lessons and puts a suggestion on the sheet. The group members then read the suggestions on their own before the group comes together for an exchange of ideas. At the end of the exercise, an agreement is listed in the middle of the sheet and used for further planning. Transfer the results obtained to the planning elements of the appendix.

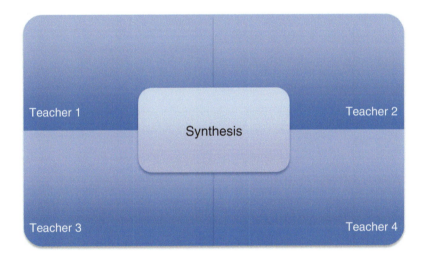

3. Plan together the evaluation of your next lessons. Create a feedback coordinate system or use an online questionnaire. Discuss the results with a colleague or colleagues. Use the following tables to capture your thoughts:

Goals	Content
Have the learners achieved the goals? If yes: why? If no: why not?	Have the learners understood the content? If yes: why? If no: why not?

(Continued)

Methods	Media
Have the methods helped the learners? If yes: why? If no: why not?	Were the media useful to the learners? If yes: why? If no: why not?
Time	**Room**
Was the time suitable for the learners? If yes: why? If no: why not??	Was the room suitable for the learners? If yes: why? If no: why not??

Teacher

Ability: in the subject? in the education? in the didactics?

Knowledge: in the subject? in the education? in the didactics?

Willingness: in the subject? in the education? in the didactics?

Judgment: in the subject? in the education? in the didactics?

My next steps

Learners

Lesson Content

Teacher Professionalism

CHAPTER

Visible teaching
Know thy impact!

"I've now been a teacher for 30 years. I have to say it still gives me as much pleasure as on the first day. Why? Because I haven't stopped planning lessons. Instead, I kept thinking: What do these learners bring? What's new in their life that I can pick up in class? What is happening in society that is worth noting? It quickly became apparent that each generation of learners is not better or worse, but different. The only thing that seems constant is the will to be taken seriously, to be able to talk, to make mistakes, and to experience a place of welcome in the school. To achieve this, constant reflection on the teaching is indispensable: What worked and what could have gone better? Throughout my life, I've made mistakes as a teacher in each of my many school hours. Dealing with this has been and still is the driving force behind my professionalization, which will never be completed."

This statement by a teacher, whom we interviewed in one of our research projects, sums up what is central in lesson planning and professionalization: know thy impact! In this chapter we would like to deal with this idea and give final hints for your further work.

The aims of this chapter

Once you have read and worked on this chapter, you should …

Surface level: Know that

- an evidence-based approach is important to everyday school life.
- mistakes in teaching have to be capitalized on.
- the Visible Learning Circle is a powerful instrument.

Deep level: Understand how

- to use evidence for professionalization.
- to reflect on the extent to which errors can be used for your professionalization.
- to comment on why working as a team is important for your professionalization.
- to develop your planning activities on an evidence-based basis.

> **The success criteria of this chapter**
>
> In order to be able to achieve the stated goals, it is necessary to understand the following content:
>
> 1. Development field "Evidence-based": The Factor of the Week
> 2. Development field "Cooperation": The Error of the Week
> 3. Development field "Collective Effectiveness Expectation": The Visible Learning Wheel

We not only concluded our book *10 Mindframes for Visible Learning* with the observation of how three girls learned a song by Taylor Swift and showed how they were highly motivated, optimally challenged, and always joyful. We also quoted Michael Jordan, one of the most successful basketball players of all time. In a commercial about his career, he says the following:

> More than 9,000 throws in my career missed the basket. I lost almost 300 games. It was up to me 26 times to make the game-winning throw, and I failed. Over and over and over again I have failed in my life. And that's why I'm successful.

In essence, teachers are no different. Teachers teach about five hours a day, five days a week, 40 weeks a year, about 35 years of their lives. That adds up to around 35,000 lessons. Not every one of these hours is successful, and none of them are flawless. How do we manage to make use of the mistakes that we make every day, which are inevitable because education is fundamentally riddled with mistakes?

In this concluding chapter we want to present three processes that have driven important professionalization processes in schools we support worldwide. As with any other method, the prerequisite for this is not just competence but also an attitude. In this respect, you not only need to know what to do but also to understand the reasons why what you do is important to you.

The three procedures pick up on the common thread woven across all the lesson planning chapters. Teacher professionalism requires:

1. **Dream**, hence the joint search and constant questioning of a vision of a school and class.
2. **Interaction and Impact**, because teachers are lifelong learners and their reaction to error shows their effectiveness.
3. **Evidence**, so as to avoid using myths in teaching but to employ evidence-based measures.

Teachers are to DIIE for – this is the essence of our approach, not only for successful lesson planning but also for successful teacher professionalization.

Dream: The Visible Learning Circle

In 2015, a multi-part documentary about a school development process made the headlines: Kambrya College was preparing to transition from being one of the worst to one of the best schools in Victoria. Founded in Brewick in 2002, just under 50 kilometers from Melbourne, the school now has over 1,000 students, of whom over 25 percent have a migration background and represent a total of over 35 nationalities – if you like, a typical school in the 21st century. Due to poor performance by the learners in national comparative tests, the school was declared a "red school" in 2008. The school management team around the headmaster Michael Muscat then set off and made contacts, including with the Graduate School of Education at the University of Melbourne. In this exchange, numerous research findings were considered and strategies implemented and evaluated repeatedly to advance the school. After a short time, the school reformed and put itself on the road to success. They focused on being transparent to students about success criteria, used assessment for diagnosis and improvement of lessons, and created a learning culture across the school that included the students, parents, teachers, and leaders.

In an intensive cooperation and exchange process, the teaching staff agreed to make key factors of successful classroom instruction visible and to focus on them repeatedly. The decision was made to focus on the factors "Goals," "Success criteria," and "Impact." But much more important is first of all the underlying process, namely that a college exchanged ideas about learning success and teaching quality, and second, the agreement to make the impact of teaching the focus of the school. Teaching quality was thus not only visible within the college but also evident to all the learners: No more lessons in which the learners are not sure why they are learning something. No more lessons in which learners are not shown what the criteria are for success. No more lessons in which the learners use media without knowing what for.

Ultimately, teaching vision led to Kambrya College's success. Teachers and school leaders worked collectively to bring about profound changes. Taking the example of Kambrya College into consideration, the following overview, which we refer to as the "Visible Learning Wheel," can offer assistance. Based on the results from Visible Learning, we have taken the following factors and translated them into the language of learners:

- Goals are one of the most effective factors to assist students to improve their learning. It is not only important that teachers have this clarity; ensuring that learners understand exactly what should be learned and when the goal is reached is crucial. That is, what does it mean to be "good enough" in this lesson? From the point of view of the learners, the following questions arise for the "Visible Learning Wheel": "What is my goal?" and "How will I know when I reach the goal?"

Visible Learning: Lesson Planning

- We have pointed out that learning cannot be sustainable without motivation. In this respect, the question "Why is this important to me?" addresses a key part of teaching. If teachers succeed in giving convincing answers, learners will be more successful in teaching. In the "Visible Learning Wheel," the following question arises from the learners' perspective: "Why is it important for me to know this?"
- The evidence for putting learners in situations where they have to show what they have learned is almost overwhelming. The learners' performance concerning the defined goals of the lesson not only show the learners where they stand but also provide feedback to the teacher about the lesson: What goals have been achieved? What content was understood? Which methods could be used sustainably? And which media are effective in retrospect? The prompt "Now I have to show what I can do!" is consequently another building block of the "Visible Learning Wheel."
- A common theme runs through Visible Learning: teachers have to see themselves as evaluators. At this point, two key aspects of successful feedback should be pointed out. First, successful feedback is not a one-way street but a dialogue. In this respect, the feedback from the teacher to the learners is important, as is the feedback from the learners to the teacher. Second, feedback is not just feedback. It proves to be particularly effective if it provides information about the further learning process from the students' perspective. For the Visible Learning Wheel, this results in the following elements: "What I want to say about the lesson!" and "What are my next steps?"

Figure 6.1

The comparative analysis of the learning cycle models mentioned in Chapter 3, section 3.6, and the structure of direct instruction revealed parallels. But also a crucial extension becomes clear, stimulated by Visible Learning, which is to introduce the "Visible Learning Wheel" within this framework. Developed from the learners' perspective, it allows them to visualize the learning and teaching. It opens up dialogue, creates commitment, intensifies the teacher–student relationship, and ensures a collegial exchange.

Interaction and impact (error culture): Error of the Week

New teachers often are socialized to stand alone in front of the class and address all the associated challenges themselves. However, this has fatal consequences for their professionalization. Teacher professionalism develops best in a culture of cooperation, in which mistakes are welcome and work is done together. In the future, teacher training must place a greater emphasis on challenge and promoting this team spirit. In the second phase, examination formats must also be changed and not be just about individual performance but also about the collective. Lessons need not be error free but also involve dealing with mistakes during the lessons. Errors should be seen by the teacher and students as opportunities to learn rather than as embarrassments to be avoided.

In order to be able to take a first step in this context, we make the following suggestion: Bring the idea to your college to take mistakes that occur during teaching every day as a starting point for discussion. For example, suggest hanging the following board in the staff room, which can be seen as an entry ticket to the dialogue:

Error of the Week

What has happened?   *How do I interpret the situation?*
What do I suggest?   *What ideas are there still?*

Evidence: Factor of the Week

So how can you bring more evidence into everyday school life? We propose to implement the Factor of the Week in your college.

Take, for example, the list of factors from the first chapter or the overview of factors in the appendix of this book. Cover up the effect sizes and start a discussion about the effectiveness of the factors at a teacher conference or in your school. You will quickly notice how teachers who do not usually talk about lessons suddenly exchange ideas about lessons and share their experiences. This is the first step toward using more evidence!

Next, uncover the previously hidden effect sizes – this will spark a discussion about how the values came about, how they align with your own experiences, and how they should be interpreted. At this point you will have won over your colleagues in participating in an evidence-based exchange about teaching quality. Coordinate among the staff which factors you would like to take a closer look at in the next six months and use intrinsic motivation. After a vote, let groups form, which then present their factor either as a poster in the teacher's room or, even better, as a short lecture at a teacher's conference. For example, the poster could answer the following questions:

a. What is the factor?
b. What is the data situation? What is the nature of the evidence?
c. What are the key results?
d. How do the results fit in with what we do at our school?
e. What can be our next steps?

Visible Learning can provide help in familiarizing teachers with the selected factors through its compilation of the most important findings from research. In addition, there are other platforms on the internet that can provide evidence for dealing with the "Factor of the Week," as well as current studies reported in the daily press. There is no shortage of empirical primary studies or international comparative studies.

If it is possible to initiate a discussion along the lines of this evidence, then sooner or later the quality of lessons will become the focus of school discussions. Over time, a new culture of collective effectiveness will develop. Your professionalization will benefit from it.

Know thy impact!

Again and again, pedagogical terms are involved in a struggle, with an emphasis on trying to throw the old overboard and embracing the new. An example is the phrase "From sage on the stage to the guide on the side – from knowledge mediator to learning companion." As important as these discussions are, in their exclusivity they misunderstand the core of pedagogy: teachers are pedagogical agents. It is not their job to convey mere knowledge or be on a stage or at the side. Rather, it is about education and therefore about people with their possibilities, but also their limits. Awakening this awareness is the central task of future teacher education. Teachers definitely teach a subject; they do not "learn" unless they learn about something.

Given the considerations outlined above, there is a need, now more than ever, for teachers to be committed to their pedagogical mission. More than ever, there is a need to reflect on education and upbringing, on education and didactics, to not succumb to the pace of the world but to master the associated challenges.

More than ever, a focus on people is required instead of constantly placing economic interests in the foreground of education. Your professionalism is in demand – know thy impact!

Exercises

Surface level

1. Explain which two interpretations "Teachers are to DIIE for" allows and what the consequences for your professionalization are.

Deep level

2. At the end of the first chapter, you were asked to create a concept map of your planning activities. As previously mentioned, we will revisit this task as we reach the end of the book. After having read this book, create a new concept map for your current planning activities. Outline on one page what is important to you in lesson planning and how you implement what is important to you. Then compare this concept map with the one from the first chapter: What has changed and what has stayed the same?
3. Please answer the following questions again and add up the points for the categories "ability," "knowledge," "will," and "judgment." Then enter the corresponding average values into the network diagram. Compare this evaluation with the evaluation from the first chapter. First reflect for yourself on what has changed and what has remained the same. Then discuss the results in a team and think about the next steps to follow from this reflection.

Ability I am in an excellent position to ...	1 2 3 4 5
... analyze the starting point of learning.	
... carry out a comprehensive planning of lessons.	
... carry out the planning with high quality.	
... evaluate the implementation of the teaching based on evidence.	

Knowledge I know exactly ...	1 2 3 4 5
... what is important in the analysis of the learning situation.	
... what is important when planning the lesson.	
... what is important for the implementation of the lesson.	
... what is important when assessing the lesson.	

Visible Learning: Lesson Planning

Will It is always my goal to ...	1	2	3	4	5
... analyze the learning situation.					
... plan the lessons comprehensively.					
... carry out the planning with high quality.					
... evaluate the lessons based on evidence.					

Judgment I am firmly convinced that ...	1	2	3	4	5
... the analysis of the learning situation is decisive for learning success.					
... comprehensive planning of the lesson is crucial for learning success.					
... high-quality implementation of the planning is crucial for learning success.					
... an evidence-based evaluation of the implementation of the lesson is crucial for learning success.					

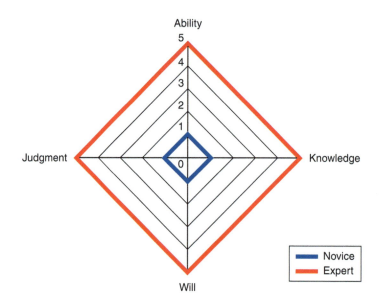

What are my next steps?

1. _____

2. _____

3. _____

Appendix

In this appendix, we summarize the key planning elements. These can be used in full or only partially. They are meant to prompt you to think about your lesson planning in an evidence-based manner and are by no means to be understood as rigid or dogmatic.

Diagnosis and discovery

Learner

Learning behavior

Strengths	Weaknesses

Working behavior

Strengths	Weaknesses

Social behavior

Strengths	Weaknesses

Family support

Strengths	Weaknesses

Lesson content

Subject matter analysis: What is the key idea of the content?

Educational analysis: What is the educational benefit of the content?

Learning analysis: What are the essential steps for surface and deep understanding?

Teacher

Ability: in the subject? in education? in learning?

Knowledge: in the subject? in education? in learning?

Will: in the subject? in education? in learning?

Judgment: in the subject? in education? in learning?

Appendix

Intervention

Learning goals matrix

General goals

Leading goals

Surface Level   Deep Level

Specific goals

Surface Level   Deep Level

Success criteria

                                        Example

Appendix

	Class discussion
approx. ___ minutes	with goals and content
	Reasons given for methods, media, time, and room
ENGAGE	Consolidate
	Challenge
	Control
	Care
	Confer
	Captivate
	Clarify

Appendix

	Class discussion
	with goals and content
approx. ___ minutes	
	Reasons given for methods, media, time, and room
EXPLORE	Consolidate
	Challenge
	Control
	Care
	Confer
	Captivate
	Clarify

Appendix

Class discussion

with goals and content

approx. __ minutes

Reasons given for methods, media, time, and room

Consolidate

Challenge

Control

Care

Confer

Captivate

Clarify

EXPLAIN

Appendix

Class discussion
with goals and content

approx. ___ minutes

Reasons given for methods, media, time, and room
Consolidate
Challenge
Control
Care
Confer
Captivate
Clarify

___ ELABORATE

Class discussion

with goals and content

approx. ___ minutes

Reasons given for methods, media, time, and room

Consolidate

Challenge

Control

Care

Confer

Captivate

Clarify

EVALUATE

Appendix

Evaluation

Goals
Have the learners achieved the goals?
If yes: why?
If no: why not?

Content
Have the learners understood the content?
If yes: why?
If no: why not?

Methods
Have the methods helped the learners?
If yes: why?
If no: why not?

Media
Were the media useful to the learners?
If yes: why?
If no: why not?

Time
Was the time suitable for the learners?
If yes: why?
If no: why not??

Room
Was the room suitable for the learners?
If yes: why?
If no: why not??

Teacher

Ability: in the subject? in the education? in the didactics?

Knowledge: in the subject? in the education? in the didactics?

Willingness: in the subject? in the education? in the didactics?

Judgment: in the subject? in the education? in the didactics?

My next steps

Learners

Lesson Content

Teacher Professionalism

References

Anderson, L. W., & Krathwohl, D. R. (2001). *A taxonomy for learning, teaching, and assessing: A revision of Bloom's taxonomy of educational objectives*. Longman.

Bakhtin, M. M. (1981). *The dialogic imagination: Four essays*. University of Texas Press.

Barrett, P., Davies, F., Zhang, Y., & Barrett, L. (2015). The impact of classroom design on pupils' learning: Final results of a holistic, multi-level analysis. *Building and Environment, 89*, 118–133.

Biggs, J., & Collis, K. (1982). *Evaluating the quality of learning: The SOLO taxonomy*. Academic Press.

Blatchford, P., & Russell, A. (2020). *Rethinking class size: The complex story of impact on teaching and learning*. UCL Press.

Bloom, B., Englehart, M., Furst, E., Hill, W., & Krathwohl, D. (1956). *Taxonomy of educational objectives: The classification of educational goals. Handbook I: Cognitive domain*. Longmans/Green.

Brophy, J. E. (1999). *Teaching*. UNESCO.

Bruner, J. S. (1966). *Toward a theory of instruction*. Belknap Press.

Byers, T., Imms, W., & Hartnell-Young, E. (2018). Comparative analysis of the impact of traditional versus innovative learning environments on student attitudes and learning outcomes. *Studies in Educational Evaluation, 58*, 167–177.

Coe, R., Aloisi, C., Higgins, S., & Major, L. E. (2014). *What makes great teaching? Review of the underpinning research*. www.suttontrust.com/wp-content/uploads/2014/10/What-Makes-Great-Teaching-REPORT.pdf

Comenius, J. A. (1657). *Didactica Magna*.

Copei, F. (1962). *Der fruchtbare Moment im Bildungsprozess*. Quelle & Meyer.

Costa, J. M., Miranda, G., & Melo, M. (2022). Four-component instructional design (4C/ID) model: A meta-analysis on use and effect. *Learning Environments Research, 25*, 445–463.

Cranford, S. W., Tarakanova, A., Pugno, N. M., & Buehler, M. J. (2012). Nonlinear material behaviour of spider silk yields robust webs. *Nature, 482*, S72–S76.

Davies, M. (2016). *Investigating the use of talk in middle and secondary classrooms* [Unpublished doctoral dissertation, University of Melbourne].

Dweck, C. (2012). *Mindset. How you can fulfill your potential.* Random House.

Gagné, R. M., Briggs, L. J., & Wager, W. W. (1992). *Principles of instructional design* (4th ed.). Harcourt Brace Jovanovich.

Gan, J. S. M. (2011). *The effects of prompts and explicit coaching on peer feedback quality* [Unpublished doctoral dissertation, University of Auckland].

Gardner, H. (2013): *Intelligenzen: Die Vielfalt des menschlichen Geistes.* Klett-Cotta.

German Education Council (1970). *Strukturplan für das Bildungswesen.* Klett.

Habermas, J. (1995). *Theorie des kommunikativen Handelns.* Suhrkamp.

Haigh, M., Ell, F., & Mackisack, V. (2013). Judging teacher candidates' readiness to teach. *Teaching and Teacher Education, 34*, 1–11.

Hart, B., & Risley, T. R. (2003). The early catastrophe: The 30 million word gap by age 3. *American Educator, 27*(1), 4–9.

Hattie, J. (2008). *Visible Learning: A synthesis of over 800 meta-analyses relating to achievement.* Routledge.

Hattie, J. (2019). *Visible Learning for teachers.* Routledge.

Hattie, J. (2023). *Visible Learning: The sequel.* Routledge.

Hattie, J., & Clarke, S. (2018). *Visible Learning: Feedback.* Routledge.

Hattie, J., & Masters, D. (2011). *The evaluation of a student feedback survey.* Cognition.

Hattie, J. A. C., & Timperley, H. (2007). The power of feedback. *Review of Educational Research, 77*(1), 81–112.

Hattie, J., & Yates, G. (2013). *Visible Learning and the science of how we learn.* Routledge.

Hattie, J., & Zierer, K. (2019). *Visible Learning insights.* Routledge.

Hattie, J., & Zierer, K. (2024). *10 mindframes for Visible Learning* (2nd ed.). Routledge.

Hattie, J., Bustamante, V., Almarode, J. T., Fisher, D., & Frey, N. (2020). *Great teaching by design.* SAGE Publications.

Helmke, A. (2014). *Unterrichtsqualität und Lehrerprofessionalität: Diagnose, Evaluation und Verbesserung des Unterrichts.* Klett.

Helmke, T., Helmke, A., Schrader, F.-W., Wagner, W., Nold, G., & Schröder, K. (2008). Die Videostudie des Englischunterrichts. In DESI-Konsortium (Ed.), *Unterricht und Kompetenzerwerb in Deutsch und Englisch* (pp. 345–363). Results of the DESI-Study. Beltz.

Humphrey, A. S. (2005). *History corner: SWOT analysis for management consulting.* SRI Alumni Newsletter. SRI International.

Imms, W., & Mahat, M. (2022). *Innovative learning environments and teacher change: Final research findings.* University of Melbourne, LEaRN. https://doi.org/10.46580/124366

Jank, W., & Meyer, H. (2002). *Didaktische Modelle.* Cornelsen.

Kahlert, J., Nitsche, K., & Zierer, K. (Eds.) (2013). *Räume zum Lernen und Lehren: Perspektiven einer zeitgemäßen Schulraumgestaltung.* Julius Klinkhardt.

Keller, J. (2010). *Motivational design for learning and performance: The ARCS model approach.* Springer.

Klafki, W. (1996). *Neue Studien zur Bildungstheorie und Didaktik – Zeitgemäße Allgemeinbildung und kritisch-konstruktive Didaktik*. Beltz.

Klieme, E. (2018). Unterrichtsqualität. In M. Gläser-Zikuda, M. Harring, & C. Rohlfs (Eds.), *Handbuch Schulpädagogik* (pp. 393–408). Waxmann.

Kounin, J. S. (2006). *Techniken der Klassenführung: Standardwerke aus Psychologie und Pädagogik*. Reprints. Ed. D. H. Rost. Waxmann.

Kruger, J., & Dunning, D. (1999). Unskilled and unaware of it. How difficulties in recognizing one's own incompetence lead to inflated self-assessments. *Journal of Personality and Social Psychology, 77*(6), 1121–1134.

Locke, E. A., & Latham, G. P. (1990). *A theory of goal-setting and task performance*. Prentice Hall.

Mager, R. F. (1962). *Lernziele und Unterricht*. Beltz.

Measures of Effective Teaching (MET) (2010). *Learning about teaching*. Bill & Melinda Gates Foundation.

Mercer, N., & Littleton, K. (2007). *Dialogue and the development of children's thinking: A sociocultural approach*. Routledge.

Meyer, H. (2004). *Was ist guter Unterricht? Mit didaktischer Landkarte*. Cornelsen.

Miller, G. A. (1956). The magical number seven, plus or minus two: Some limits on our capacity for processing information. *Psychological Review, 63*, 81–97.

Nida-Rümelin, J. (2013). *Philosophie einer humanen Bildung*. Körber.

Nitsche, K., & Zierer, K. (2013). Raumgestaltung. In K. Zierer (Ed.), *Leitfaden Schulpraktikum* (pp. 83–87). Schneider Verlag Hohengehren.

Nuthall, G. (2007). *The hidden lives of learners*. New Zealand Council for Education Research Press.

Pfost, M., Hattie, J., Dörfler, T., & Artelt, C. (2014). Individual differences in reading development: A review of 25 years of empirical research on Matthew Effects in reading. *Review of Educational Research, 84*(2), 203–244.

Puentedura, R. R. (2018). *SAMR: A brief introduction*. http://hippasus.com/rrpweblog/archives/2015/10/SAMR_ABriefIntro.pdf

Ridley, M. (2010). *The rational optimist. How prosperity evolves*. Fourth Estate.

Sanders, B., & Zierer, K, (2019). Schulisches Feedback: Welche Formen von Feedback verwenden Lehrende und wie lernwirksam schätzen Lernende diese ein? *Pädagogische Rundschau, 73*(6), 589–601.

Schiller, I. S., Remacle, A., & Durieux, N. (2022). Effects of noise and a speaker's impaired voice quality on spoken language processing in school-aged children: A systematic review and meta-analysis. *Journal of Speech, Language, and Hearing Research, 65*(1), 169–199.

Scriven, M. (1967). The methodology of evaluation. In R. Tyler, R. Gagné, & M. Scriven (Eds.), *Perspectives on curriculum evaluation* (pp. 39–83). AERA monograph series. Rand McNally.

Swanson, E., McCulley, L. V., Osman, D., & Scammacca Lewis, N., & Solis, M. (2017). The effect of team-based learning on content knowledge: A meta-analysis. *Active Learning in Higher Education, 20*. https://doi.org/10.1177/1469787417731201

Tuckmann, B. W. (1965). Developmental sequence in small groups. *Psychological Bulletin, 63*, 384–399.

Van den Bergh, R. A., & Beijaard, D. (2010). *Feedback van basisschoolleerkrachten tijdens actief leren: De huidige praktijk*. ORD-paper. Enschede.

von Schiller, F. (1856). *The parasite or the art to make one's fortune*. Bohn's Libraries, London.

Webb, N. J. (1997). *Criteria for alignment of expectations and assessments on mathematics and science education*. Research monograph number 6. CCSSO.

Wilber, K. (2001). *Eros, Kosmos, Logos*. Eine Jahrtausend-Vision.

Zierer, K. (2010). *Alles prüfen! Das Beste behalten! Zur Eklektik in Lehrbüchern der Didaktik und des Instructional Design*. Baltmannsweiler: Schneider Verlag Hohengehren.

Zierer, K (2019). *Putting learning before technology!* Routledge.

Zierer, K., & Seel, N. (2012). General didactics and instructional design: Eyes like twins. A transatlantic dialogue about similarities and differences, about the past and the future of two sciences of learning and teaching. *SpringerPlus, 1*, 15. 2012. https://doi.org/10.1186/2193-1801-1-15

Zierer, K., Werner, J., & Wernke, S. (2015). Besser planen? Mit Modell! Überlegungen zur Entwicklung eines Planungskompetenzmodells. *Die Deutsche Schule, 4*, 376–396.

Zierer, K., & Wisniewski, B. (2019). *Using student feedback for successful teaching*. Routledge.

Index

Page locators in *italic* refer to figures.

ACAC model 15, *16*, 45
achievement tests 23–24
acoustics, classroom 99
acrostics 24–25
air conditioning, classroom 99
attitudes: expertise as a symbiosis of competence and 8–12, 15, *16*, 43–45; reflecting on own 46–48

Bakhtin, M. M. 111
Biggs, J. 40, 65, 67
Bloom's taxonomy 65–66, 68; revision 66–67
Bruner, J. S. 76

class as a whole, analysis of 28–32, *29*; group cohesion 30–32, *31*; group composition 32; group development 29
class size 28
classroom design *see* space planning
classroom management 110, 112–114
classrooms, open vs. traditional 28, 82, 97
cognitive task analysis 75, 76–78
collective intelligence 49–50
Collis, K. 40, 65, 67
color scheme, classroom 98–99
competence: didactic 43–44; expertise as a symbiosis of attitudes and 8–12, 15, *16*, 43–45; pedagogical 43–44
"The Confidence Builders" 84, 109–110, 114–115
content analysis 37–42, *38*; educational analysis 39–40; exercises 41–42; learning analysis 40–41; subject matter analysis 38–39

content planning 74–80; cognitive task analysis 75, 76–78; exercises 79–80; forms of representation 76–77; motivation strategies 77; scaffolding and situated learning 75–76
"The Controllers" 110, 112–114
cooperative learning 59, 86, 90
curricula impacting learning performance 37–38

diagnosis and discovery 19–53; DIIE model 12–14, *13*; learner analysis 21–37; lesson content analysis 37–42; summary of key planning elements 142–143; teacher professionalism analysis 42–53
dialogue-based speech 111–112
"The Dialogue Promoters" 84, 109, 110–112, *111*
didactic competence 43–44
didactic hexagon 60–61, *60*
didactic reduction 40–41
digital media: choice 92; effectiveness 59, 90–95, *91*; shortcomings in software programs 93; upgrading schools 93
DIIE model 12–16, *13*; *see also* diagnosis and discovery; evaluation; implementation; intervention
direct instruction 103
discussion guides 78, 85
disruption, dealing with class 113–114
DOK (Depth of Knowledge) model 65, 67–68
domains of Visible Learning 5, *5*
Dunning–Kruger effect 27
Dweck, C. 114

e-asTTle tool 23–24
educational analysis of lesson content 39–40
effect: distribution 4, *4*; size 3–7
error culture 112, 137
Error of the Week 137
evaluation 117–132; digital feedback 128–130, *129*, *130*; DIIE model *13*, 15; exercises 131–132; feed up/back/forward perspectives 125, 126; feedback from student to teacher 126–130, *127*, *128*, *129*, *130*; feedback levels 120–125, *121*; feedback matrix 126; formative 120, 129; summary of key planning elements 150–151; summative 120
"The Evergreens" 83
exercises: evaluation 131–132; goal planning 73–74; implementation 116; learner analysis 34–37; lesson content analysis 41–42; lesson content planning 79–80; lesson planning 17–18; media planning 95–96; method planning 88–89; space planning 102; teacher professionalism 50–53, 139–141; time planning 107
expertise: distinguishing 7; as a symbiosis of competence and attitude 8–12, 15, *16*, 43–45

Factor of the Week 137–138
factors, Visible Learning 4–7
family factors impacting learning 32–34
feedback 120; coordinate system 127, *127*; digital 128–129, *129*, *130*; feed up/back/forward perspectives 125, 126; formative 120, 129; levels 120–125, *121*; matrix 126; and performance level of learners 124–125; process level 122, 123, 124, 125, 126, 128; self level 121–122, 123; self-regulation level 122, 123, 124, 125, 126, 128; from students to teacher 126–130, *127*, *128*, *129*, *130*; summative 120; targets 127, *128*; task level 122, 123, 124, 125, 126, 128; on Visible Learning Wheel 136, *136*
5E model 104–105
formative evaluation 120, 129
furniture, classroom 98

Gagné, R. M. 64
Gardner, H. 7, 39
German Education Council Taxonomy 67, 68
goal planning 60, 61–74; aligning teaching methods with 85; exercises 73–74; formulation of goals 63–65; "Goldilocks Principle" 68–69; learning goal hierarchy 62–63, *62*; learning paths 69–70; success criteria 69, 70–73; taxonomies 65–68
goals on Visible Learning Wheel 135, 136, *136*
"Goldilocks Principle" 68–69
group, analysis of classroom 28–32, *29*; group cohesion 30–32, *31*; group composition 32; group development 29

Habermas, J. 44
Haigh, M. 81–82
Hart, B. 33–34
Hattie, J. 2, 3, 5, 8, 10, 12, 14, 15, 28, 33, 38, 43, 46, 49, 61, 68, 71, 73, 84, 85, 87, 88, 90, 110, 115, 120, 123
Herberger, S. 118
home factors impacting learning 32–34
homework 32–33, 59, 87–88, 105

IKEA effect 115
implementation 108–116; "The Confidence Builders" 109–110, 114–115; "The Controllers" 110, 112–114; "The Dialogue Promoters" 109, 110–112, *111*; DIIE model *13*, 14–15; exercises 116; strategies and impact on learning 59
intervention 54–107; content planning 74–80; DIIE model *13*, 14; goal planning 61–74; implementation strategies 59; learning strategies 57–59; media planning 90–96; method planning 80–89; space planning 96–102; summary of key planning elements 144–149; teaching quality models 59–61, *60*; teaching strategies 57; time planning 102–107
IRE response method 110–111

Jordan, M. 134

Kambrya College, Australia 135
Keller, J. 77
know thy impact! 8, 138–139
Kounin, J. S. 113

language development at home 33–34
Latham, G. P. 64
learner, analysis of 21–37, *23*; classroom factors 28–32, *29*; exercises 34–37; factors and influences in learning 22; family factors 32–34; framework conditions 27–34; learning and working behavior 25–27; prior knowledge 23–25; skills in working with peers 25; social behavior 30–32, *31*

Index

learning analysis of lesson content 40–41
learning and working behavior 25–27
learning cycle models 104–105
learning goal hierarchy 62–63, *62*
learning paths 21, 69–70, 87
learning strategies 27
learning strategies and impact on learning 57–59
learning styles 27
lesson content analysis 37–42, *38*; educational analysis 39–40; exercises 41–42; learning analysis 40–41; subject matter analysis 38–39
lesson content planning 74–80; cognitive task analysis 75, 76–78; exercises 79–80; forms of representation 76–77; motivation strategies 77; scaffolding and situated learning 75–76
lesson design 104–106
light and lighting, classroom 99
Locke, E. 64

Mager, R. 63–64
media planning 90–96; choice of media 92; effectiveness of digital media 59, 90–95, *91*; exercises 95–96; shortcomings in software programs 93; upgrading schools 93
meta-analyses 2–6
method planning 80–89; "7 Cs of Effective Teaching" 86–87; "The Challengers" 83; "The Confidence Builders" 84; "The Dialogue Promoters" 84; "The Evergreens" 83; exercises 88–89; homework 87–88; primacy of goals in 85; self-regulated learners 84–85
mistakes 44, 112, 137; digital media and revealing of 94; Error of the Week 137; Michael Jordan on making 134
monologue-based speech 110, 111
motivation: and feedback 121; strategies 77; on Visible Learning Wheel 136, *136*
multiple intelligences 39

networks 9–10
"not yet" 114–115
Nuthall, G. 127

open vs. traditional classrooms 28, 82, 97

parents, working with 32–34
pedagogical competence 43–44
peers, power of 25, 59, 100, 112
planning and designing models: ACAC model 15, *16*; DIIE model 12–16, *13*; dimensionality 12; improving lesson planning and design 10–12; levels of understanding 12; perspectivity 11; reputation with teachers 16
pre-service teachers' readiness to teach 81–82
prior knowledge: making visible 104–105; procedures for determining 23–25
problem-based learning 59
process level feedback 122, 123, 124, 125, 126, 128
psychological tests 25, 30
Puentedura, R. R. 94

questions: to assess readiness to teach 81–82; *why* 33, 77, 112

relationships, teacher–student 84; feedback and 121–122; strengthening 109–110, 114–115
representation, forms of 76–77
retention of learning 27, 63
rewards, use of 121
Risley, T. R. 33–34

SAMR model 94–95, *95*
Sanders, B. 123
scaffolding and situated learning 75–76
Schiller, F. von 97
seating plans 100–101, *101*; and disruptive students 114
Seel, N. 10, 11
self level feedback 121–122, 123
self-regulated learners 84–85
self-regulation level feedback 122, 123, 124, 125, 126, 128
"7 Cs of Effective Teaching" 59–60, 86–87, 92, 110–111, 112
SMART goals 64
smiling 115
social behavior 30–32, *31*
social media 25, 91
sociograms 30–32, *31*
SOLO (Structure of Observed Learning Outcomes) 40, 65, 67, 68; learning intentions success criteria 71–72
space planning 96–102; acoustics 99; air-conditioning and ventilation 99; arrangement of tables and chairs 98, *98*; co-design 99–100; color scheme 98–99; exercises 102; furniture 98; light and lighting 99; open vs. traditional classrooms 97; seating arrangements 100–101, *101*; structuring 99
structural characteristics 6, 7

subject matter analysis of lesson content 38–39
success criteria 39, 56, 70–73; differentiated 69, 87
summative evaluation 120
SWOT analysis 48

tables and chairs, arrangement of 98, *98*
task level feedback 122, 123, 124, 125, 126, 128
teacher professionalism: analysis of 42–53, *46*; dream of Visible Learning Circle 134, 135–137, *136*; error culture 112, 137; evidence-based measures 7–8, 134, 137–138; exercises 50–53, 139–141; expertise as a symbiosis of competence and attitude 8–12, 15, *16*, 43–45; know thy impact! 8, 138–139; processes required for 134; reflecting on own attitudes 46–48; SWOT analysis 48; teachers as activators, evaluators and change agents 7–8; team players 45–46, 48–50, 137; "Three Es" of expertise 7
teacher–student relationships 84; feedback and 121–122; strengthening 109–110, 114–115
teacher talk 110–112, *111*
teaching characteristics 6, 7–8
teaching quality models 59–61, *60*
teaching strategies and impact on learning 57
team players, teachers as 45–46, 48–50, 137

10 Mindframes for Visible Learning 2, 8–10, 43, 134
"30–million–word gap" 33–34
time planning 102–107; direct instruction 103; exercises 107; lesson design 104–106

ventilation, classroom 99
Visible Learning 2–8; *10 Mindframes for Visible Learning* 2, 8–10, 43, 134; domains 5, *5*; effect distribution 4, *4*; effect size 3–7; exercises 17–18; factors 4–7; meta-analyses 2–6; structural characteristics 6, 7; teaching characteristics 6, 7–8
Visible Learning Wheel 135–137, *136*
visible teaching 133–141; Error of the Week 137; exercises 139–141; Factor of the Week 137–138; know thy impact! 8, 138–139; professionalization processes 134; Visible Learning Wheel 135–137, *136*
vocabulary development at home 33–34

Webb, N. L. 65, 67
why questions 33, 77, 112
Wilber, K. 44
Wisniewski, B. 129, 130
working and learning behavior 25–27

Zierer, K. 2, 5, 8, 10, 11, 12, 15, 33, 38, 43, 46, 49, 60, 90, 94, 95, 98, 123, 129, 130

For Product Safety Concerns and Information, please contact our EU representative GPSR@taylorandfrancis.com Taylor & Francis Verlag GmbH, Kaufingerstraße 24, 80331 München, Germany

Printed by Integrated Books International, United States of America